C000157436

GROWTH AND POSITIVE THINKING MINDSET

Complete Step by Step Guide on How to obtain The Best Mindset for Growth and Positive Thinking to Achieve Success in Life and Live Your Dreams

Improve Yourself Series Book 2

GARRETT REDFIELD

TABLE OF CONTENTS

Introduction.. 1

Chapter 1: Listen to your thoughts.. 3

Chapter 2: Can You Imagine? 22

Chapter 3: Using Your Toolkit to Set Mental Markers...... 34

Chapter 4: Love 43

Chapter 5: Nutrition, Food & RecipeS 58

Chapter 6: Consciousness and Mindfulness 81

Chapter 7: The Road Ahead 102

Chapter 8: Visualize Success! 115

Chapter 9: Sunrise - Sunset... 125

INTRODUCTION

We all have our dreams, and so often they are never fully realized. Why is this? Well, the common ground we all share is that we think, and most of us do not know how to control these thoughts or organize our relentless inner voices. This inner voice has been called our thoughts, our self-talk, or simply our mental dialogue. Our minds create what would appear to be a ubiquitous conversation, but does this "conversation" influence us?

If we say, "yes it does," then does in not mean that those thoughts and inner conversations could both help or hinder our real-life aspirations and plans for the future? It does indeed.

This book proposes a process by which our inner thoughts might be utilized as a powerful tool towards our very aspirations and dreams for the future. The book is written around the intention of one goal. To use both our physical and our mental energies to obtain a winning mindset, for growth and positive thinking, in order to achieve success in our lives and live our dreams.

In nine easy to understand steps, this book takes us forward while keeping a steady cadence and understanding of where we are, where we want to be, and how to get there.

The book delves into meditation, visualization processes, and how to use our imaginations, how to "take stock" along the way, and how to keep moving forward and not lose our momentum.

It teaches us to keep our mental inertia, pushing us ahead no matter what barriers arise.

If you follow the steps put forth in this program, you should enjoy a high probability of success and have fun doing it. How to develop relationships, deal with problematic alliances, and make each day a step further. Even suggestions regarding relationship tools such as throwing dinner parties or creating other potentially self-propelling events and processes.

When you do achieve your goals and reach your dreams, you will find, in this program, the tools you need to maintain that success. There are many stories revealing how success was gained only to be lost again. This book teaches you the entire program from inception to the crucial information that will keep you at the top after you reach that pinnacle. Please enjoy! In addition, if you find this book helpful or enjoyable, consider leaving a review on Amazon to let other readers know!

CHAPTER 1: LISTEN TO YOUR THOUGHTS

Step One: Assign a letter grade to your Mindset!

All those conversations going on inside your head are a lot like listening to all the stations on the radio at once. So, in our mind, we have a lot of noise and activity, and we want silence. On one end of this spectrum, we have utter chaos, and on the other end, we might find someone like a trained remote viewer or someone who is highly skilled in meditation. Also, some athletes have been known to speak about how they get psyched up for their event. They speak about how they believe that concentration is the ability to think about nothing. Of course, this would mean that they are able to clear their mind of everything leaving only the task at hand. You might not think you go around talking to yourself, but in truth, we all have our inner voice, which continually tells us all sorts of things. Mental responses to outside influences, attitudes you are accepting or rejecting, or judgments you are making based on what you see and hear around you.

Where do all our thoughts come from anyhow? Well, our thoughts come from the Cerebrum, which is the large, outer part of the brain. This is where reading, thinking, learning, speech, vision, hearing, and other senses come from.

You must control your inner voice and all of its white noise distraction. The way in which you can do this is by assigning that inner voice a "distraction grade!" That's right. Just like back in school. If you perform poorly, you get an "F" If you perform with honors, you get an "A."

You will assign whatever grade you want in the beginning. Go ahead and give it an F if you think it is an F. As you see yourself advancing, you will notice the "noise" growing dimmer. Then, give your pesky inner voice a D or even a C if you think it has earned it. Get the picture? This will work. If you like, write down the grade you are currently working with on a whiteboard or just stick it up in a prominent place on your wall, on a piece of printer paper with push pins. Write the letter grade with a magic marker and make it huge so you always have to look at it. You will want a better grade, and you will work towards it each and every day. You will win!

You may not know this, but I'm going to give you a secret weapon to use exclusively against limiting and negative thought processes. That's right! We are going after those inner voices who don't like your team and don't want you to achieve your dream! Let's just call this "Team _____!" (Your first name goes there!)

Say it! Say it often! Here it is. Endorphins! We'll talk about them later, but if you call them up, you win. It's that simple!

We need a pathway to a clear mindset in order to think only those productive thoughts that will lead us down the road to success in our lives and in our dreams. Fortunately, there is a very simple way to do that. Like the athlete, we begin by listening to our thoughts in the course of a day. For learning purposes, let us call this, "your inner voice." Notice how many times your inner voice tells you something negative. This could be anything from you dropping the soap in the shower that morning to not being able to find a parking space when you arrive at your job. When those things happen, did you hear your little voice tell you something like "this always happens to me" or "I never get a break.?" Don't worry, we all have our inner voices and believe me, most of us hardly notice how unproductive they are. Those negative statements you hear are the result of ingrained patterns related to our own beliefs about self-esteem, security, money people, and everything we have known. When we get in an emotionally negative state, we might begin to see ourselves as less attractive or having less value. This could occur in such amplitude that it could lead to eating disorders such as overeating or a lack of appetite and not eating enough, and often not even caring about it. So, you see how those negative thoughts and emotions might just be much more severe than you may have initially believed.

And there is more. Your negative mental state could have a considerable effect on those around you, those who may rely on you or you may need in your life to rely on. Switching to positive thinking is a simple matter of making a conscious effort. To rid your mind of negative thoughts, you need not fight them, but rather merely replace then with positive ones. Be in the moment. Thinking about your past or worrying about your future can make you anxious. Indeed, the more negative your behavior becomes, the worse you will end up feeling. Other potentially good ways to alleviate negative thinking is by trying new things or exercising more. Shift your perspectives and make your breakdowns, breakthroughs! There are challenges at every pace of our lives. We all have them! How we handle them is key. Often it might help to do something unreasonable.

Something out of your "comfort zone." This will awaken your senses to new, different, and better, and those are three good things we can always use. You may be in a rut and not even know it. Doing something unreasonable will surely tell you, and it might be fun. Shake it up a bit. Step out of your "safety zone."

Whether you are consciously aware of it or not, most of the time, your thoughts are in control of you and how you are feeling at any given moment. That being the case, it would be great if you could have more control over what you were thinking so that you could change the way you were feeling at any time. Well, you can! Here are a few things you can do to get started.

Stand up and breathe deeply. Most of us would be quite surprised to learn that shallow breathing was limiting our mental processes and affecting our overall health. Take a deep breath. Breath in all the way until you can't take in any more air and then pull in just a little more. Then, slowly let it out. At the bottom of your breath, push a little farther. Puff hard and try to exhale just a little more air out of your lungs. Repeat this entire process three times and then walk around a bit to get your body moving.

Be certain to check that you are not daydreaming and that you are in the moment. Be here now! Always, be in the moment. If you do this daily, it will become easier, and you will find yourself more aware of your surroundings and more in touch with your activities and with others around you. You will love how this feels! Good to be alive and good to achieve!

Don't do any one thing for too long. Of course, this would not apply to your job as we all have a job description, but in your off time, try to break up your time to keep your mind active.

The importance of exercise cannot be overemphasized in this area as it gets more oxygen to the brain and has a wonderful clearing effect called endorphins. Endorphins pass signals, acting as neurotransmitters between different neurons. They serve to either incite or cease a specific signal to another neuron, making them an integral part of the central nervous system. So, what does that sound like in nonscientific terms? You may have heard someone tell you about exercise, sex, or perhaps even spicy food giving them "endorphin rushes."

Studies conducted in the 1970s have shown us a way in which opiates affect our brain. Drugs such as morphine or heroin can severely impact a cell's receptors. As those cells are mostly located in a person's brain or spine, these drugs can interfere with the pain signals and their transmission from one cell to another. But the very existence of these receptors might actually be the consequence of another naturally produced body substance, one that resembles opiates quite closely.

When you are thinking positively, and when you smile, your brain releases endorphins, giving you a good feeling energy boost. Positive thinking can not only reduce your stress at work, but it can also change the way you view stress, which has far-reaching effects on your life.

Some years ago, I had a fully Carbon Fiber, 21-Speed Road Bicycle, and was working on doing what cyclists call "A Century." That would be a very long and grueling bike ride of 100 or more miles. While training on my very lightweight and awesome bike, I would begin slowly, and after about twenty or thirty minutes, my mind would literally shift gears. I would get this amazingly light feeling, and as I looked down at my legs pumping away, I simply couldn't feel anything. I don't mean loss of feeling but rather "legs on auto-pilot!" It really was quite unbelievable, and I think the ultimate mindful activity. I loved every minute of it! What I was experiencing was a feeling of wellbeing as endorphins were being triggered. I lost track of time, giving myself over to the cadence of my legs and the rhythm of my breathing.

Other popular ways to generate endorphins would be to eat chocolate, to drink wine, or have sex. Also, meditation can manifest this amazing phenomenon, but one of the easiest and most fun ways to generate endorphins is simply to have a good time and to laugh.

So, what other foods and activities can trigger endorphins?

- Sniff some vanilla or lavender
- Take a little ginseng
- Take a group exercise class
- Listen to music

- Eat something spicy
- Eat an Avocado
- Eat pure Cacao
- Eat Egg Yolks
- Take a B Vitamin Booster
- Eat Leafy Greens

Then there is the case of Endorphin Meditation. If you are reading this, then chances are you are somebody who wants to advance your well-being. Meditation is a gift to humanity and what a pity our medical doctors do not build on its fantastic principles. With Endorphin Meditation, emptying your mind might not be as much of a challenge as filling it with thoughts that bring you joy. However, it is the latter challenge that will give you a sense of pleasure. Cortisol, adrenaline, and even stress hormones will be put to rest by these endorphins, which will then change your body chemistry for the better. I found that it really was that easy to feel marvelous and I had to ask: why hadn't I used this method in my life before?

Physical Health benefits of meditation

• Meditation will not only make you smarter, but also help with memory, concentration, self-awareness, self-restraint, and many other things, all that by making your brain increase in volume and density.

• Meditation will help your brain function better by increasing the blood flow to it, making it stronger.

• Meditation will also reduce your body's production of cortisol. This hormone is generated by environmental stress and can raise your levels of anxiety in a sudden manner, as well as negatively impact your immune system.

• Meditation helps with high blood pressure, reducing the amount of pressure that is inflicted on your heart or major arteries.

• Meditation can also help with your brain's organizational functions and adaptability. This is called neuroplasticity, an aspect of the brain that can help with learning and education.

• Meditation positively affects your mood by increasing the number of neurotransmitters, such as serotonin and dopamine. These neurotransmitters have been proven to change your mood drastically, and a lack of serotonin, in particular, can lead to depression.

• Meditation will help you rest and relax,

particularly after a stressful day.

• Meditation will reduce your body's stress levels, which will have a meaningful impact on your health, happiness, and immune system.

• Meditation can also help with your physical wellbeing. By relieving stress, meditation will also reduce the muscle tension caused by it, a tension that, in many cases, can lead to a variety of medical issues.

• Meditation will also help your body release more melatonin, and reduce its production of cortisol, will make you look younger and slow down your body's aging.

Everyone's brain is different, and different responses to endorphins can produce a slightly different result. There is no exact answer to what you will experience. Some minds are more open to suggestion, and some are stubborn. Many people have absolutely "Wild Experiences," while others have more mild effects.

How to get started in Meditation

To know what meditation is, or what meditation can do for you, simply close your eyes for one minute and pay attention to the specific thoughts in your mind. Pay close attention to them. Make a note of how many different thoughts pass through your head in one minute.

Notice how many of those thoughts are sheer nonsense, and how many of those thoughts are simply rewinds of thoughts you have seen innumerable times. Wouldn't it be nice to go beyond this constant disturbance of the mind to enjoy a perfectly peaceful and quiet moment? That's exactly what meditation can do for you.

Meditation is a way for you to systematically quiet your mind so that you can really relax.

Every night our bodies relax totally, so why shouldn't our minds be able to tune to and relax the same way? The word Meditation originates from the Latin word meditari, which means "ponder," as meditation is actually in a sense a way in which to ponder life.

Meditation is a simple and beautiful way of exploring our lives. It is one of the most scientific ways of getting rid of our daily stress and anxiety. Apart from offering the practical benefits of helping us to stay calm and relaxed, meditation also opens up pathways to our rich inner life. Initially, meditation is a challenge, but later, it becomes a great source of relaxation. Eventually, it helps us to answer some of the most important questions we have about our lives.

The best meditation posture is one where you can

relax easily without falling asleep. Any posture that can help you to relax and stay awake at the same time is a good meditation posture.

Meditation posture need not and should not be complicated. It is not necessary to sit in the traditional cross-legged position. You can comfortably sit in a chair and even use a backrest.

Sit in a comfortable posture with your spine erect but not stiff, and keep your head slightly tilted upwards to avoid falling asleep. You can place your hands on your lap.

Always remember that the best meditation posture is one where your body is relaxed, and your mind is alert.

Begin slowly, with controlled and even, breaths. Watch each breath as it flows in and out of your body. If a thought comes into your mind, just let it go and continue to watch your breath. After what seems like every other breath, keep bringing your mind back to your breath.

Watching your breathing without your mind wandering is the hardest thing you will ever do! Even experienced meditators have to keep bringing their minds back to the breathing.

Watching the breath keeps you in the moment and helps to keep you from engaging with the constant babble of your mind. When thoughts ramble across the stage while you're attempting to watch your breath, let them go. Don't entertain them, and certainly don't argue with them; it's almost like the mind wants us to be distracted from meditation.

Meditation is quiet, and the mind is noise. That's easy to see if you will just close your eyes for 30 seconds and make a note of everything your mind thinks of while your eyes are closed. It's amazing just how much of it is nonsense and re-runs!

The objective of meditation is to be fully aware but fully relaxed. With continued practice, this gets easier. The first time you meditate will be an experience like you've never had. You'll follow all the directions to get into the most comfortable "meditation-like" position that you can get in, close your eyes, and begin breathing in a controlled manner.

Then you begin watching your breath. You will wonder which part of the breath to watch, but it really doesn't matter whether you are aware of your breath coming in the nostrils, going into your lungs, or exiting your body, just watch the breath; this will keep you in the moment.

Here's where the mind kicks in: It's going to ask you questions like, "What you are doing, why are you doing this," and then it will remind you of eleven other things you should be doing rather than wasting your time sitting. Just notice how active your mind gets when you're sitting quietly and watching it.

You're going to let those thoughts flow on down the stream, and then you're going to go back to focusing on the breath. In and out, in and out.

If you got into trouble in the 4th grade, here's where your mind will bring that back up; just let it go. Come back to the breath.

There's probably a song playing somewhere in the background as well; just ignore it. That's part of the clutter that you're trying to step away from. If you didn't get into a comfortable position to start with, this is when your legs will let you know they are not comfortable. Your back will start hurting if it's not supported properly, and something will itch.

It's okay to shift positions if you aren't comfortable, and it's okay to scratch that itch if it's driving you crazy. This is all a learning process, and you'll figure out which positions are most comfortable for the amount of time you spend sitting.

You can use a timer when you first begin sitting, just to avoid interrupting your meditation to look at the clock. Don't stop before the timer goes off!

Your first-time meditating is probably going to be very frustrating, but it does get better. It's just like learning any new skill; the first few times you do it you're not so good at it. Eventually, you become more comfortable and can go deeper. "Deeper" is when you can actually sit with no thoughts. This is nothing short of the most amazing experience ever.

The regular practice of watching the breath and continuing to come back to the breath, again and again, is really just a way to get away from the mind. Once you've practiced getting away from the mind enough, there comes a time when you're able to use it as a tool whenever you want and put it away when you want just to be.

Meditation is not a journey to an end. Meditation is a journey through life. As a matter of fact, if you get distracted by some pre-conceived end result, your mind has already won!

Your mind will constantly taunt you into thinking that you don't know what you're doing, and you're wasting time. Just keep meditating. What you're trying to do is to quit letting the mind have control of every moment of your life; to learn how to use it when you want to, and keep it quiet the rest of the time. The more you sit and watch your thoughts, the less they come around. When we meditate, help ourselves in creating benefits that will have a profound and long-term impact on our lives. We set ourselves up for success by lowering our stress levels, by knowing what hurts us or what brings us joy, by establishing more meaningful connections with people, and by improving our concentration. But mostly, we help ourselves by being positive and by being kind to our minds and bodies. Meditation will not solve every single problem in your life, but it will help you attain a state of mind in which finding solutions to problems will seem much simpler, like less of a chore than ever before. Think about how easy it would be to make decisions about our personal lives or about our relationships if only we got rid of the stress and negativity clouding your mind. With meditation, you can become a more introspective person, and this will be the most crucial tool for any challenges you may face. All you need is patience and a comfortable place to meditate.

The mindfulness that comes along with meditation will help you recognize your own emotions and thought processes a lot better. It can help you analyze what your mind is thinking and take a step back to be able to think better, to feel better, and to actually be able to focus on what's important to you. Distractions are a common occurrence, but they are the exact opposite of a mindful spirit. Mindfulness will help you take the wheel on your brain and thoughts. It will help you be present in the moment, as opposed to letting your mind wander and get lost on future or past occurrences, or to simply lose focus on what really matters. By being in the present, you will be able to take control of your life and increase your productivity. Meditation and mindfulness will help you understand yourself and the way you work. If you think of your brain as your most powerful tool in life, think then of meditation as a guide to help you master it and make the most of it.

Although we've reviewed the basics for breath meditation, there are many mindfulness techniques that are centered around elements other than breath, making you focus on a different point of your body. This focal point could be ambient noise in your environment, for example. The main takeaway from all this is that, in any type of meditation, it is our minds that control everything. It controls what we think and the way we act upon those thoughts, which is why it is important to be mindful. There are several strategies to change the way your mind works.

The Habit of Mindfulness

95% of our behavior is subconscious, according to different estimates. Many of our habits are composed of neural networks that allow our mind and brain to comprehend the hundreds of thousands of sensory inputs our body experiences every moment of our life. Brain signals are then established as shortcuts to allow us to function better, but they are efficient to the point where a few outside factors can trigger a signal and make us execute on our habits as a default instead of being able to break them.

Mindfulness, on the other hand, is completely different. It allows us to take control of our actions and enables us to have intentional reactions to different inputs. The more you practice meditation, the better you will become at making conscious choices. Doing something new and deliberate stimulates neuroplasticity and helps generate new neurons that have not yet been "programmed" by these shortcuts and habits.

Our intentional actions are based on what we think (or what we know) is good for us, whereas habits are just ways of being able to function without thinking too much. When we need our mind to be able to make mindful decisions, behavioral design has been proven effective. With this, your subconscious triggers are stopped by obstacles, whereas your consciousness is free to do what it wants.

This process requires a lot of time and effort, especially from someone who just started meditating, but we do have some tips regarding that.

• Establish reminders. Triggers can help you remember to meditate. A good example of this would be putting your yoga mat close by or setting your meditation cushion on the floor in front of you so that it becomes easier for you to remember what you have to do.

• Renew your reminders regularly. Whatever trigger you decide to use to remind yourself of a new action or reaction to having, it is easy to succumb to habits after a week or two. This is why you should keep your triggers different and fun. Keep them interesting so that they can allow you to stay on your toes.

• Create new patterns. If you know Boolean code, you might be familiar with If-Then-Else. This is a way of creating patterns, in which you set a reaction (Then) for a specific occurrence (If) and a reaction if that occurrence doesn't happen (Else). This can be as simple as "If I get a work email, then take a breath before reading it."

Once you feel like you have mastered the basics of seated meditation, you can start looking into different techniques. Meditating while walking or lying down is fairly popular. Be sure to use your breath as the focal point still, so that it is easier to follow. Here is a list of different forms of meditation.

Body Scan Meditation

For Body Scan meditation, you need to be seated with your feet on the ground. Shoes aren't necessary, just wear whatever you're comfortable in. Then proceed to scan your body. You want to start with your toes, checking in with every part of your body as you scan all the way up to the crown of your head. Don't worry about what you think of your body, just make sure that you are aware of it, that you are in touch with your body.

During this, you want to focus on every small part of your body. Linger for a few seconds on every section, and make sure you are paying attention to different sensations in those specific areas. When you begin to get distracted, just bring your mind back to the last part you remember scanning. Remember to stay focused, but don't panic if you lose track of the scan. Practice makes perfect!

Some people fall asleep during body scans. If this happens to you, take a long and deep breath to reawaken yourself. Change positions as well, into something that won't facilitate your sleep, and then begin again.

Walking Meditation

Long gone are our nomad days, and most of us spend our time sitting at home or work. We have to integrate physical activity into our days for our health, but this can be difficult if you already spend time meditating. Don't let this get in the way of your physical health, however. Instead, find ways of bringing meditation into your daily routine, and this can be done easily if you enjoy walking.

Choose a natural place, such as a nearby park for example. Place your hands on your stomach, behind you, or just let them hand on your sides.

• Count your steps! This can serve as a focal point for your meditation

• Pay attention to the way your body moves, guided by your legs. Notice the way it sways, or the way you carry yourself

• Don't be frustrated if you get distracted, simply guide your mind back to walking as many times as you need

• Stay safe and alert, and don't neglect the environment around you.

CHAPTER 2: CAN YOU IMAGINE?

Step Two: Imagine you are where you want to be. Do this often!

We are surrounded by self-help books, self-improvement programs, and life enhancement videos, and everyone tells us that they have the winning formula for success. Just taking it all in can be daunting at best, and some of us just want to back away and go hide under the bed! Make it simple! Notice everything you think and do that offers little or nothing towards your goals and then find a mental clearing that will provide you a place to work on this. That place is your imagination, and you own it.

So just where does our imagination come from? Imagination and reality flow in different directions in the brain. The occipital lobe, located in the lower back section of your brain, is where imagination comes from. The visual cortex, which processes visual information and helps us see, is contained in this lobe. Above the occipital lobe is the parietal lobe, whose main function is to differentiate information our body is subject to though our five senses, such as vision, touch, and sounds. The parietal lobe lies above the occipital lobe, and its primary function is to integrate sensory information, such as vision, but also touch and sound. Our bodies are an amazing machine, and the brain can do unbelievable things if we just eat right, get lots of exercise, and accept mental challenges. Use your imagination with intention and be inventive and original. Think about inventing new things and coming up with stories or writing songs. Great artists, musicians, and writers are normal people just like you and me. Try using your imagination every day, and you can develop a unique solution to a problem or issue.

Einstein once said imagination is more important than knowledge. Looks like he was thinking well beyond his time. So, in the end, creativity improves things, but imagination is at the heart of breakthroughs. In today's world, you must ask questions, pick a topic, and really learn all about something new and different. Become an expert and share your knowledge by teaching others.

Be playful and try new things. When you are playful, your mind is allowed to roam free, and your subconscious can start working. When you play, let your mind wander and give your subconscious time to work. Think about your future. Let your imagination think five years ahead, into your successful like. What does this life look like to you? What is success to you? Write down your answers to these questions, and then try to elaborate. How did you attain that successful stage? What steps did you take to get there? Ask yourself, "What was the first step you took to move toward your goal?" or "What was some of the early obstacles, and how did you move past them?"

You can also come up with your own ideas. Pick a random household object, whatever is closer to your reach as you read this book. Make a list our of these objects, and then challenge yourself into finding different uses for them. Set yourself a short time limit to come up with a long list. Just have fun with it no matter how silly it might seem. It's good for the imagination, and that is good for your future.

You can also try toppling, a process in which you generate new words using free association. Every word, however, must have a different kind of connection to the last one. Your sequence could then be "chocolate-bar-band," with your connections being "chocolate bar" and "bar band." Remember though; the links must be different.

Stretch the limits of your imagination by engaging with who you would picture yourself interacting with in the first place. Your friends are so similar to you that it builds a comfort zone, which is good, but it doesn't allow you to expand your horizons.

Don't stop editing. Everything can always work slightly better. Ask people you trust to play Devil's Advocate about why your idea won't work and then defend or reject the project.

All of these things keep the brain working and the imagination active. Have fun with it.

Draw something! If you are concerned about skill, don't be. Everyone can doodle, and what you do doesn't need to be perfect. You don't need to show it to anyone; it is simply meant to help you imagine. Turn people into sketches, make cartoons out of comical situations in your life, use shapes and symbols to express yourself. Anything works.

Make a collage. Look for photos and paragraphs of text in your local newspaper or a magazine. If you find any that relate to a problem you want to solve, cut it out and glue it to a poster. Leave it on a wall where you can think about it more. You will find new ways of thinking about old problems.

Build something. If you don't have a garage full of power tools, just get some Legos, Tinker toys, an Erector Set and go crazy. You can build a tabletop train set! Be open and aware, and your imagination will prosper.

Where do you see yourself in one year? In five years? Imagine it, and it will be!

Why is our imagination so important? So many reasons why!

• Imagination ignites passion

• Our imagination and thoughts create our future

• Imagination stimulates creativity and innovation

• Imagination is magical
• Imagination is childlike and fun
• Imagination is relaxing

"Most folks are about as happy as they make up their minds to be." - Abraham Lincoln

What is positive thinking? Although many might

interpret this as meaning being constantly positive and idealistic, without caring or bothering to solve any problems, positive thinking is actually a way of having a more positive and brighter outlook on the challenges you face.

This doesn't mean ignoring problems and bad things. It simply means that you should look at the positive side of any bad situation and try to see the best outcome. View things under a positive light, and you will find yourself with some peace of mind.

People might think of positive thinking as an explanatory style, a way you have of explaining things that have happened in your surroundings. For example, some people tend to give themselves credit for any good event they took part in, while blaming others for bad ones. To these people, negative events can seem temporary and infrequent.

On the other hand, certain people tend to blame themselves for bad situations, and refuse to take credit for good ones. To them, negative events are something they are used to. They are long-lasting and frequent. This can obviously affect your state of mind negatively.

Positive thinkers tend to fall in the first category, but the explanatory style will vary from one situation to the other.

Health Benefits

Positive thinking can have a great impact on your health, and this idea has been perpetrated by self-help books and online articles. These tend to describe positive thinking as the remedy to every illness or difficulty, but research has indeed found that positive thinking and optimistic attitudes can have very serious benefits on your health.

One of the major clinics in the US gave this assessment:

A positive mindset is linked to a wide range of health benefits, including:

1. Longer life span
2. Less stress
3. Lower chances of depression
4. Increased immunity to the common cold
5. Enhanced stress management skills
6. Lower risk of cardiovascular disease and its related deaths
7. Increased physical wellbeing
8. Increased physiological health

According to a study conducted on 1,558 adults, positive thinking can help diminish frailty in the senior years. Positive thinking has many benefits, but what is it that makes it have such a meaningful impact on a person's health, be it physical or mental?

Researchers think that positive thinking could lead to lower levels of stress among the people who practice it. These people also tend to live better lives in general, as a result of a healthy diet, increased exercise, and the elimination of unhealthy behaviors in their lives.

Positive Psychology

It is important to note that positive thinking is not the same as positive psychology. The former means an individual has a positive outlook on life, whereas the former means an individual is optimistic. While these two may sound similar, it must be said that optimism lacks the necessary realism an individual needs in life, something positive thinking doesn't. Optimism is having unfounded beliefs that everything will turn out the way we want them to, whereas positive thinking means making the most out of bad situations.

There are many misconceptions about positive psychology, which we will try to clear up by shedding light on the origin of the movement and what exactly it is.

The most popular definition of positive psychology is that it is "a scientific study of what makes life most worth living." It is considered a scientific approach to psychology, with a particular focus on positive aspects rather than negatives. It has for aim to create good things and opportunities for the individual that practices it, as opposed to simply fixing what has already gone wrong. "Strength, optimism, life satisfaction, happiness, wellbeing, gratitude, self-compassion, self-esteem and self-confidence, hope, and elevation" are all described as being topics that are at the center of the field of positive psychology.

More examples of Positive Psychology are as follows:

Express your heart: The number of friends you have doesn't matter nearly as much as having a few close friends who you can express yourself to. Sharing the way you feel with those who are close to you makes a difference in your levels of happiness. Making your friendships stronger can be done by what some call "active-constructive responding," which is the act of being an attentive listener and knowing how to respond. Showing your friends that you are genuinely interested in their stories and feelings goes a long way, and they will do the same for you.

Cultivate kindness: Caring for others can lead to increased happiness and lower the chances of depression. This can be done not only through volunteering but also by lending a helping hand to those around you. Look at the people in your environment, be it at work or in school or in your neighborhood and see if anyone would benefit from your help. This will make them want to help you and others in the future.

Altruism: Although your main reason for taking care of those around you might be the simple desire to help, and it could come from an entirely selfless place, altruism will still have a positive impact on you. According to several psychological studies, volunteering, or simply just helping, can lead to "better psychological wellbeing." This wellbeing then translates into satisfaction in your own personal life, which will increase your happiness. It also will help those around you, not only psychologically and mentally, but many times also physically.

Caring for others, through any kind of action, is indirectly correlated to positive thinking and happiness, particularly among older adults.

While younger adults might not benefit from the

same levels of happiness, constant and regular volunteering can increase the youth's psychological wellbeing, particularly if it is done through a long period of time. As opposed to simply volunteering because of school requirements, or to boost your college application, long-term volunteering that is motivated by an individual's desire to help and moral responsibility can be much more beneficial and satisfactory.

People who benefit from volunteer activities organized and participated in those same activities are also more likely to experience more happiness through it. As opposed to this, people who were helped but remained passive in the activity did not benefit from the same amount of increased happiness. In fact, some experienced depression following volunteering.

The results of these studies are hard to prove, mostly due to the lack of hard data when it comes to people's intentions when volunteering, or people's participation in volunteering activities. But while we can't identify an exact association between the two, we can safely assume that there is a positive correlation. A randomized trial was therefore conducted with two groups of adults, one engaging in volunteering for three months, while the other did not. The results of this trial found that "those who volunteered scored higher on indices of mental wellbeing than those who did not." These effects were also said to have lasted long after the trial period of three months had ended. This goes on to prove that not only does volunteering have a positive effect on an individual, but also that this effect is long-lasting.

Volunteering is seen as the result of an individual's caring nature. However, psychological researchers are trying to determine what comes into play in this caring nature. What is it that drives some people to be caring, and others to not be? Is it the result of nurture, in which altruistic individuals come from caring families and communities? Is this caring behavior perhaps triggered by a particular event in which an individual is motivated to do good after seeing another person do good, or after being on the receiving end of a good deed? How do culture and beliefs come into play into all of this? Altruism largely depends on context, and there is not one single answer to these questions.

Positive psychology is the analysis of what gives us purpose. What is the meaning of life, and how do we, as human beings, go from mere survival to actually living and flourishing; these are the questions that positive psychology aims to answer. While other fields of psychology are centered around mental illnesses and disorders, and in finding a cure for them, positive psychology treats with neurotypical individuals and examines how they can be happier in their day-to-day lives. But positive psychology works in tandem with abnormal psychology, not as a replacement for it. According to the late Christopher Peterson, a pioneering researcher in the field, the positive psychology movement is founded on three maxims: "What is good in life is as genuine as what is bad.... What is good in life is not simply the absence of what is problematic.... And third, the good life requires its own explanation, not simply a theory of disorder stood sideways or flipped on its head." In positive psychology, there is an emphasis on meaning, not just on fleeting happiness and warm fuzzy feelings. Many people have tried to find a cure for human misery. Online articles, books, gurus, everything is trying to find and point to a way of fixing things. But to find out which remedy will be more efficient, a scientific approach to the question will always be preferred. Positive psychology is a topic that is more and more researched as time passes. These studies can then provide us with a clear plan of action to increase happiness and bring us peace of mind. This, in turn, has a positive impact on other fields, such as counseling and life-coaching. This book aims to do just that: compile and write down that plan of action.

To me, positive psychology is so interesting because it provides an underpinning for our concept of a positive mindset, which is why I wrote this book. Thank you again for reading about this all-important topic for today's society. And once again, if you liked the book, please leave a review on Amazon. We'd love to hear from you.

CHAPTER 3: USING YOUR TOOLKIT TO SET MENTAL MARKERS

Step Three: Control your thoughts!

You can control your thoughts with your toolkit. Well now there's a silly idea, right? A Mental Toolkit? Well actually this is a very GOOD idea and here's why.

When the plumber finds a leaky pipe, he knows he must replace it to stop the leak. How does he do that? He reaches into his toolkit and grabs the right tool. My Dad used to tell me "use the right tool for the job at hand," and he was always right!

When unproductive or "junk" thoughts enter our minds uninvited, fix them with your very own mindtools. First, think of a bell ringing each time you hear negative or unproductive words. This can be your mental alarm system to keep you alert, so you stay on the program.

By identifying them as leaking "IN" and deleting them, setting a mental reference marker at the sound of the bell, and moving ahead, we CAN choose only good thoughts and toss the bad stuff out. Good thoughts beget good results. Always visualize the good in others and in yourself. This will lift your energy and force you to improve.

Health Benefits of Thinking Positively

Let's talk about the research being performed on this topic and see how positive thinking has an effect on our health. Studies show that personality traits such as enthusiasm and confidence versus depression and uncertainty can have a significant impact on several aspects of an individual's health and wellbeing.

Combining a happy disposition to the practice of positive thinking is key in being able to manage stress more effectively. A more efficient method of stress management can lead to a variety of health benefits in whoever practices it. If you tend to be gloomy and exhibit hopelessness, it does not mean you can't change and end up with a bright sunshiny positive outlook. Even the worst can mend!

Research reveals that people with adequate methods of stress management and positive thinking benefit not only from lower rates of depression and distress but also from an increased life span. Moreover, immunity to the common cold and better cardiovascular health can be found among these individuals. Psychological and physical wellbeing, as well as coping skills, are all elements that improve greatly because of positive thinking.

Positive thinking can lead to all these health benefits among the people who engage in it. Coping with stress can be a great way of diminishing any harmful effects of stress on your psychological and mental health, and these better coping skills can be attained by having a positive outlook on life.

According to research, individuals that are more positive and cheerful than their average counterpart have healthier lifestyles. They benefit from exercise, a nutritious diet, and a lack of harmful vices such as drugs and cigarettes.

Identifying Negative Thinking

How to take stock: Is your outlook on life positive or negative?

• Filtering: If you find yourself focusing and emphasizing the negative aspects of a problem instead of paying attention to the positive ones, you may be negative thinking. This is the case for people who come home after completing all their work tasks quickly and, instead of taking time to think about the compliments they received for your work, start planning out ways to work even harder the next day.

• Personalizing. If you feel that you tend to put the blame on yourself after a problem occurs, you are negative thinking. This is the case for people who assume their friends no longer like them or want to be around them when plans for an evening are canceled.

• Catastrophizing. If you find yourself always expecting the worst, you are negative thinking. This is the case for people who anticipate their entire day will go wrong, simply because they got the wrong order at their morning coffee shop.

• Polarizing. If you see things as either black or white, you are a negative thinker. This is the case for people who cannot see a middle ground and view themselves as failures unless they're perfect.

Focus on Positive Thinking!

Create a winning formula in order to transform your negative outlook into a more positive one. This requires time, effort, and commitment, but the process itself is quite simple.

Here are some ways in which you can start engaging in positive thinking:

• Identify areas to change. To engage in positive thinking, pinpoint aspects of your life that you tend to think negatively about. This can be work, family, even something as simple as diet. Focus on one small area on which to apply positive thinking, and you will feel more confident about the process.

• Check yourself. Take breaks during the day to evaluate your state of mind. Be constantly mindful. If you find that you are thinking negatively, try to find a positive aspect to those thoughts.

• Be open to humor. Laughter is the best medicine! Laughing and smiling will make you feel better, even if you don't feel particularly happy. Try to find comical situations in your environment and try to make people around you laugh as well. This will help reduce your stress and make you happier.

• Follow a healthy lifestyle. Exercise doesn't necessarily have to mean going to the gym. It can sometimes be as simple as taking a walk outside. Set aside half an hour of your day to focus on being physically active. This will positively affect your mood and help decrease your stress levels. Paired with a nutritious diet, it can also fuel your body and mind to do things you want them to do.

• Surround yourself with positive people. Cut out people in your life who do nothing but increase your stress level. Surround yourself by people who make you feel confident about your life, who can support you through difficult periods, and on whom you can rely on for advice and feedback. Do not forget to maintain those relationships.

• Practice positive self-talk. Don't say, or even think, things that are not positive. Do not belittle yourself or others and remember always to be gentle and kind to yourself. Thinking negatively of yourself will only make positive thinking harder. Instead, replace negative thoughts about yourself with positive affirmations.

Practice Positive Thinking Each and Every Day!

You won't become a positive thinker overnight. It takes patience and diligence, but soon, you will find that you accept yourself more and that you criticize yourself less. You will learn to appreciate the world around you.

Positive thinking will help you cope with stress constructively, which will, in turn, bring you a variety of health benefits.

CHAPTER 4: LOVE

Step Four: If you could choose success over failure, you would not choose failure!

Life is a series of choices. You do not need to make concessions in order to make one choice over another. You choose freely because it is your choice.

What you feel about your dreams is love. Love is our truest strength, and with love comes action. Love is strength. Keep love in your heart, and never ever give up your dreams. Always choose love! When you go with love in your heart, the road ahead will be clear.

After all, are we not but one species on our little planet? A view from space should make this crystal clear as we will not see race; we will not see gender or judge by language or attitudes. We hold a powerful element in our collective hands in the concept of unity. And in unity is love.

Your success is built upon the long road up to the mountain, and you must be responsible to yourself and to others. Your destination will, in all likelihood, present the need for solid relationships and alliances. This can only be accomplished with unity. Unity is the most powerful force in the universe. Without unity, there is only chaos.

As you climb higher each day towards your goals, remember only to build relationships and never burn them. Do not use people but rather enroll them. Allies and alliances will be key all the way to the top.

You may not be aware of it, but your display of positive thinking and its cultivation can have a huge influence on your general well-being. Also, keeping your mind full of positive energy does impact the way you connect with those around you.

You will also find that cultivating a positive attitude can help you come up with solutions to the problems of everyday life as well as solutions to questions which invariably arise in the business arena. Additionally, it will assist you in understanding the perspectives of those around you, and maintaining a sense of unconditional respect for them. This is a key factor in the foundations of business creation. So, chances are very good that you will need these factors as you move forward towards your dreams and goals.

Your new positive self will also contribute greatly to you in the area of romantic relationships. Your ability to identify the value of an opposing perspective will bolster your emotional intimacy.

Through this, an increase of empathy for your partner will become helpful in times of misunderstandings or the escaping of a thoughtless word misplaced or unintended.

We all know how difficult being around someone with a negative and gloomy outlook can be. We choose, whether voluntarily or involuntarily, to be around people who are enthusiastic and uplifting. This is because being in the presence of thy type of individual is truly energizing and most pleasant. If you radiate positive energy, your loved ones and colleagues will love being around you, and this is how great organizations are born.

Positive thinkers also tend to focus more intensely on solving issues rather than creating or worrying about them. Research has shown that positive thinkers are much more equipped to deal with stress and conflict in a way that is rational and efficient. Providing solutions to problems always resolve issues and smooth out the way forward, whether in business or personal affairs.

For many of us, positive thinking can sound like the optimal solution to our problems, and like the best way to get rid of negativity. It is perceived as a gentle term that seems too idealistic actually to be practical; similarly to persistence and determination. However, these perceptions are quickly changing, as more research is done. Psychologists are revealing that positive thinking is more than just faking a happy attitude in order to convince yourself nothing is wrong.

Positive thinking can add genuine value to your life by helping you build and improve on your own skills, and cope with the negative effects of stress.

There are many examples of this. One of them is of a cougar leaping out in front of you as you are walking through a desert. Your brain's immediate reaction might be fear. Since your brain is programmed to have a specific reaction to that kind of emotion, your "instinct" might be to run away, without considering any other factors. You are focused solely on your fear and how to reduce it, on escaping the cougar. These negative thoughts have an impact on the way you react to situations. Your best option would be to climb a tree, to pick up something to use as a weapon, or to simply stay calm and hope the animal does not notice you. Instead, you run, knowing perfectly well that the cougar will outrun you.

This might be a useful instinct, and it might seem rational to think that way, as you are unlikely to encounter a cougar in a city. However, the main takeaway from this is that you are not making the decisions based on the problems you are facing. Your subconscious is making decisions based on your negative thoughts, without consideration for any other factors or options.

When you get into an argument with someone else, the negative emotions you experience are anger and resentment. This clouds your thinking and could lead you to say things you don't mean. In a similar fashion, being overwhelmed with stress at the beginning of a busy day at work might interfere with your actual performance and could even go as far as paralyzing you and stopping you from being able to start anything. Thinking negatively about your body can also make you not want to go to the gym, and it can make you feel like you are unmotivated, no matter how much motivation you actually have.

In each of these scenarios, your brain stops thinking about your environment and the factors in it that it should consider, and focuses instead on your negative thoughts, in the same way it did in the cougar example. These negative emotions are what prevent you from thinking outside the box, from thinking of solutions that could be more helpful, and from making rational decisions. Instincts are not a bad thing, but it is always more beneficial to take the time to process all the information you can and act accordingly.

What positive thoughts do to your brain

When you have positive thoughts and emotions, your brain releases endorphins that can prompt you to feel even more positive emotions. You may start feeling joy, contentment, satisfaction, and even love. These emotions then open up your mind for broader, more positive thinking. However, this is only the beginning. Positive thinking can have even more impact later on.

Building your positive thinking skillset

While positive emotions and feelings are good, even when felt for only a short period of time, these are not the only benefits of positive thinking. The benefit is what derives from those emotions: the ability to gain and improve your skills so that you can then apply to different aspects of your life.

Take, for example, a happy child. This child will go outside, play with their friends, run around, and engage in physical activities with them. Thus, the child grows more agile and athletic. They can also gain communication and social skills faster than an unhappy child. Games can also lead them to be more curious about the world about them. Simply by being happy and acting on that emotion, the child can gain physical, social, and creative skillsets.

Emotions may not last for long periods of times, but skills do. A child that is athletic will be healthy and strong and might get a scholarship to attend college for playing a sport they enjoy and excel at. A child that is social will have an easier time later on networking with their peers and superiors and might earn promotions quicker. A child that is creative will develop new ways of expressing themselves through art, leading to a more positive mind.

Negative emotions do the exact opposite. They put barriers between an individual and the acquisition of skills, and instead make them focus on their immediate problems, without helping them find solutions.

But if positive thinking can help with so many aspects of life, how can you become more positive?

Increasing your positive thinking mindset

What can be done to develop your positive thinking and be able to improve your skills?

By now, you probably know what makes you happy. This could be a hobby, a relationship, or a goal. It could be something as simple as listening to your favorite album. Anything that sparks joy around you can help you be more positive.

Here are three things you can do that can also bring you joy:

1. Meditation: People who meditate tend to display more positive emotions than their counterparts, according to research. These people can, therefore gain and build more valuable skills.

Mindfulness and a sense of purpose in life are things that can be obtained through meditation, as is an improved immune system.

2. Writing: Writing about positive experiences can help improve your mood. A research conducted on two groups of 45 students, one who wrote about their positive experiences for three months, and one who didn't, proved this.

The first group of students profited not only from a better mood but also from increased health, demonstrated by fewer visits to the clinic.

3. Play: Try and set aside some time in your day to play. In the same way that you would schedule meetings and appointments into your calendar, schedule a play period, make it a priority, and stick to it.

You can use the hour to create, or simply have fun in any way you want. Think about the last time you actually spent time having fun, without feeling like it was holding you back from doing more productive things. Once you make playing a priority and actually carve out time to do it, it becomes less of an inconvenience, and more of a natural part of your day.

Don't use this hour to simply lay down browsing the Internet. Take that time to catch up on your favorite show, call a friend you haven't talked to in a long time, or maybe do something creative. Allow yourself to feel happy and positive emotions through things that actually make you happy, as opposed to things that just make you satisfied.

Happiness vs. Success

Happiness can be the result of any achievement, such as getting promoted, moving forward with a relationship, or winning a championship. Achieving a goal you set for yourself will undoubtedly bring you joy, happiness, and satisfaction. But success on its own doesn't always guarantee happiness.

We often think, "if I get this one thing, then I will be set and never want for anything else."

We also think, "Once I achieve this, I will be content and won't need to aim higher."

You should never let your happiness rely on an arbitrary goal you set for yourself. Instead, try to increase your happiness now in order to gain and build the skills that will allow you to reach your goals.

In the end, success won't always bring you happiness, but happiness will bring you success.

This is something that has been proved by research. People who are happy tend to move upward in their lives. Their happiness enables them to develop new, useful skills that can later be applied in their road to success. This success then brings more happiness, and the cycle continues.

Where to go from here

Positive thinking isn't just an arbitrary term in order to make people feel good about themselves. Happiness is great, but it is also critical to build and develop the skills you need to achieve goals, be it in your career, your education, or your personal life.

Finding happiness does more than simply bring you temporary emotions and lower your stress levels. Doing things that make you happy, such as playing a sport or finding a craft, can do a lot more for you.

These moments in which you are happy are moments in which you can engage in positive thinking to see how you can apply your experiences to your future, how you can develop skill sets that will benefit you later on in your career, or how you can motivate yourself to go further.

To make this brief: be positive, find happiness, invest time in what brings you joy. Success will develop itself.

Some people tend to classify their feelings of love in a relationship as addiction, and you've probably done it too. This is actually correct. Studies reveal that the chemical process the brain goes though when falling in love is the same as the one that takes place during addiction:

"Love is a chemical state of mind that's part of our genes and influenced by our upbringing. We are wired for romance in part because we are supposed to be loving parents who care diligently for our helpless babies. Romantic love both exhilarates and motivates us. It is also critical to the continuation of our species. Without the attachment of romantic love, we would live in an entirely different society that more closely resembled some of those social circles in the animal world. The chemicals that race around in our brain when we're in love serve several purposes, and the primary goal is the continuation of our species. Those chemicals are what make us want to form families and have children. Once we have children, those chemicals change to encourage us to stay together to raise those children. So, in a sense, love really is a chemical addiction that occurs to keep us reproducing."

Romantic love is an important part of a person's life, regardless of culture and environment. Culture might generate different ways of displaying affection, but the essential feeling remains.

What makes us fall in love?

Everyone one of us has a "type." This is the combination of characteristics we look for in a partner, and it is how we ultimately differentiate between a person we want to pursue a relationship with, and one we don't. But many things come into play with regards to our type.

Appearance:
Studies have found that we have a tendency to pursue people who are physically similar to our parents, whereas others have found that we might instead be attracted to people who look like ourselves.

Personality:
Similarly to appearance, we also have a tendency to be attracted to people with personalities that remind us of a parent, or of people who were close to us during our childhood, because they are familiar.

Pheromones:
Pheromones are still an important topic when discussing love. The word "pheromone" is derived from the Greek words "pherein" and "hormone," which translate to "excitement carrier." We can observe pheromones in animals as scents found in their bodily fluids. These scenes indicate that they are sexually active and will attract animals of the opposite

sex for mating. An organ in an animal's nose, called the vomeronasal, is what detects pheromones.

In humans, the existence of pheromones has been constantly debated, as has their effect on sexual attraction.

For example, sea urchins release pheromones in the water, signaling to nearby urchins in the colony that they are ready to mate, and prompting them to "eject their sex cells." But while this process seems completely straightforward in animals, the same cannot be said for humans.

At some point in your life, you might have felt the sweat on your brow, a tickle in your groin, a warm flush to your face, and a shot through the heart when you first laid eyes on your amour, but that initial "love at first sight" feeling is actually thanks to a chemical response triggered by the brain.

According to several studies, "love at first sight," or the act of laying your eyes on someone you are incredibly attracted to for the first time, triggers your brain into producing three chemicals: dopamine, oxytocin, and opiates. These chemicals are what make you fall instantly in love.

Researches have devoted their careers into analyzing the chemical process of falling in love, and what our brain goes through when it experiences romantic passion. Dopamine has been found to be the most powerful chemical in the equation, leading to feelings of pleasure, excitement, and exhilaration.

CHAPTER 5: NUTRITION, FOOD & RECIPES

Step Five: Stay Away from Poison Boxed Food!

What if I told you there were Super Foods that would make you a super person? It's true!

The top of my list contains Blueberries, Walnuts, Turmeric Powder, and Quinoa. Also, on my list are Green Tea and Mint Tea. Any type of Mint Tea will do, but I love Peppermint!

We're going to cover a few of the super foods that are available to all of us in this chapter.

These are super foods you will get a super boost from, and they will, of course, assist you with your quest for the positive mindset. Also, look for some great recipes later on in this chapter.

But before we get to the super foods, we should

cover a huge problem in our culinary lives.

Super Bad Foods! Pretty colorful boxed frozen artificial chemical-laden processed worthless empty plastic foods found in every grocery store across America. You don't want to know what's really in these monstrous offerings. Since this is a self-development book, I thought you should know!

Processed Foods and What You Consume

Any food that is altered during its preparation, counts as processed food.

Processing can mean anything, from freezing, baking, and drying, to chemically altering food.

This process increases the levels of salt, sugar, and fat in food. You know the ones. Cereals, boxed dinners, canned food full of sodium, sweets of every kind and the list goes on.

Highly poisonous toxic processed food has taken over roughly 60% of the American diet.

Here is a list of some of the usual suspects.

1. Palm Oil

Trans fat is created by blasting hydrogen into regular fats, such as corn or soybean turning them solid. These trans fats are what make packaged food remain fresh and have a longer shelf-life without distributors worrying about it rotting. A lot of junk food contains trans-fat, and eating them can increase your LDL cholesterol and triglycerides while lowering your HDL. Trans fats are also the cause of many cardiovascular diseases, as they can lead to clogged arteries and heart attacks. You should strictly avoid palm oil and other trans fats and eliminate any food that contains them. Fry food is often cooked in these, so it is better to fry your food yourself to watch what you eat.

2. Shortening

Shortening or partially hydrogenated oil is also trans fats, and they should be avoided when you do your groceries. They will not only lead to blood clots and obesity, which can cause cardiovascular diseases, but they will also put you at risk of metabolic syndrome. If you need to keep fats in your diet as part of a cooking, try choosing healthier monosaturated fats. These can be olive oil, canola oil, or anything containing omega-3 fatty acids.

3. White Flour, Rice, Pasta, and Bread

These foods consist of whole grain that has been refined and stripped of its nutrients. While this can extend the shelf life of the product, fiber, vitamins, and minerals are also removed in the process. This makes them easy to digest for most people. However, they can also have a severe impact on your insulin and blood sugar, making them spike up. If you suffer from diabetes or are at risk of it, stay clear of these products. You can easily replace them with whole grains, such as whole-wheat bread or brown rice.

4. High Fructose Corn Syrup

Out of all refined grains, high fructose corn syrup (HFCS) is the most dangerous. We might be consuming less refined sugar than we were 40 years ago, according to surveys, but our HFCS consumptions have increased 20 times over. This is the main source of calories for most Americans, according to Tufts University, as it is present in almost every food we consume. HFCS can increase your fat-storing hormones, making it easier for people to gain weight. Under all circumstances, you should steer clear of this product.

5. Artificial Sweeteners

Chemicals that are used to replace sugar are actually more dangerous for us. Products such as Equal (aspartame), Sweet'N Low (saccharin), or Splenda (sucralose) are marketed as diet-friendly, but they are not. They simply trick your brain into neglecting the fact that more sweetness comes with more calories. As a result of this, people eat sweets and candies with sweeteners without realizing their consumption.

6. Sodium Benzoate and Potassium Benzoate

These benzenes are the chemicals added to carbonated drinks to prevent them from molding them. Benzenes are actually carcinogens than can cause severe damage to the thyroid. When benzene builds up after a bottle or can of soda is left in the heat, it can rise to dangerous levels. Don't put yourself at risk.

7. Butylated Hydroxyanisole (BHA)

Although the FDA has ruled it as safe for consumption, BHA could still potentially be a carcinogen. Similarly to benzenes, they prevent food from spoiling. However, it has been deemed a "major endocrine disruptor," meaning it can have a severe impact on your hormones. This chemical is present in many foods, as well as packaging and cosmetics.

8. Sodium Nitrates and Sodium Nitrites

Sodium nitrates and nitrites are both preservatives, often added to processed meats and deli meats. They are also carcinogens, as research has led up to believe that they could be a cause of colon cancer and diabetes. Include fresh, organic meat cuts in your meals to be safer.

9. Artificial Coloring

The artificial colors blue 1 and 2, green 3, red 3, and yellow 6 have been associated with a variety of different cancers, such as brain and kidney cancer. Scan the label on the food you buy, especially if you have kids that eat colored treats, and look out for these chemicals in order to keep yourself and your family safe.

10. MSG

MSG stands for monosodium glutamate, which is known as a flavor enhancer. Glutamates are natural and are present in many unprocessed foods, but MSGs are processed and devoid of any kind of protein. While the specific effect of MSG is uncertain, high levels of glutamate can have a negative impact on your brain chemistry. Avoid these products and use spices to add flavoring to your food yourself.

You should limit or if you can, remove processed food from your kitchen and from your diet.

I realize everyone can't just change everything overnight. However, if you begin to see the health benefits from eating Organic Farmed foods or at least fresh veggies and good legumes and other great products such as Quinoa, it is really easy to dump the poison in the box and make your mind and body love the difference.

Moving on, I thought you might like to know a little more about those chemicals you have been eating if you do eat processed food. Here are the most offensive of the list.

Aspartame. In 2017, a major study revealed that aspartame caused an increased risk of cardiovascular disease and could lead to obesity. Smaller studies are easier to dismiss, but the research in question was done of over 400,000 thousand adults that had been followed for a decade, giving the result more credibility.

There are no benefits in consuming diet or low-sugar processed foods. Sodas such as Diet Coke contain artificial sweeteners, similarly to other processed foods. Not only do these foods bring no benefits, but they are also the cause for weight gain in many people and can lead to metabolic syndrome or type 2 diabetes, especially in people whose families have a history with these diseases. Aspartame and other sweeteners can be found in anything, so make sure you read the label.

Here are some other toxic chemicals found in the food we purchase.

Sodium nitrate: Carcinogen added to stop bacterial growth in different types of meat.

Sulfites: Chemical used to maintain freshness in foods. Can lead to breathing problems in certain individuals.

Azodicarbonamide: Chemical causing asthma, often found in burger buns or bagels.

Potassium bromate: Carcinogen added to different types of bread during baking to increase their size.

Propyl gallate: Carcinogen found in foods containing high amounts of fat.

BHA/BHT: Carcinogen used to extend the shelf life of foods containing fat.

Propylene glycol: Chemical added to dairy products to thicken them. Also known as antifreeze.

Butane: Carcinogen added to processed meat such

as chicken nuggets to give them a fresher taste.

Monosodium glutamate (MSG): Chemical causing headaches in humans and having been found to cause nerve damage and seizure in animals. It is used as a flavor enhancer.

Disodium inosinate: Contains MSG, used predominantly in snacks.

Disodium guanylate: Contains MSG, also used in snacks.

Enriched flour: Toxic ingredients combined into a refined and processed starch, used in snacks.

Recombinant Bovine Growth Hormone (rBGH): Genetically engineered growth hormone used on cows in order to boost their milk production. Contains the carcinogen IGF-1.

Refined vegetable oil: Combination of oils and trans fats used in cooking and frying. The omega-6 fats it contains are linked to heart disease and cancer.

Sodium benzoate: Carcinogen that is also linked to DNA damage. Often added to salad dressings and sodas to keep them fresh.

Brominated vegetable oil: Poison leading to organ damage and birth defects. Although it is present in many soft drinks, it is not required to be listed on the label, so do your research.

Propyl gallate: Proved to be carcinogen to rats. Is found in packaged foods such as soup mixes and frozen dinners. Although it has been deemed safe by the FDA, it is banned in some countries.

Olestra: Used to replace natural fats in snacks. The

body is unable to absorb this substance, which can lead to digestive problems and cardiovascular diseases.

Carrageenan: Carcinogen, also able to cause ulcers. Used to thicken prepared foods.

Polysorbate 60: Carcinogen often found in baked goods, acting as a thickener.

Carnauba wax: Carcinogen found in chewing gum and in food glazing.

Magnesium sulphate: Has been linked to cancer in laboratory animals, carcinogen.

Chlorine dioxide: Linked to tumors and hyperactivity, found in bleaching flour.

Paraben: Linked to breast cancer and hormone disruption. Often used to reduce molding in foods.

Sodium carboxymethyl cellulose: Carcinogen often used in salad dressings as a thickening agent.

Aluminum: Carcinogen often found in foods and their packaging.

And now for the good news!

Food products that enhance wellbeing

I like to take a Turmeric Powder drink in the mornings. I mix up the Turmeric powder with some good quality water, fill the glass ¾ of the way up and then add milk to the top. This mix needs a lot of stirring to get it smoothed out and on its own, it tastes pretty bad but here's how I overcome that. Before I add the Turmeric Powder, I add a packet of a fruit flavored daily vitamin product which makes the finished drink actually quite palatable.

Here is a little info on Turmeric: While Indians have known this for a long time, research is starting to prove some facts about turmeric, namely, that it contains compounds with medicinal properties. This spice coming from the turmeric plant, has a bitter taste that is usually added to curries and mustards to enhance the color or the flavor. Turmeric root, that is, the root of the plant, also has medicinal properties. It contains curcumin, a potent antioxidant of a yellow color.

Turmeric can be used for a variety of diseases, such as "arthritis, heartburn (dyspepsia), joint pain, stomach pain, Crohn's disease and ulcerative colitis, bypass surgery, hemorrhage, diarrhea, intestinal gas, stomach bloating, loss of appetite, jaundice, liver problems, Helicobacter pylori (H. pylori) infection, stomach ulcers, irritable bowel syndrome (IBS), gallbladder disorders, high cholesterol, a skin condition called lichen planus, skin inflammation from radiation treatment, and fatigue"

Turmeric can also be used for more minor illnesses, such as headaches, colds, rashes, and menstrual problems. It's also been used to treat depression, cancer, Alzheimer's disease, and diabetes.

You can apply this spice to your skin to treat rashes or ringworms, swellings, acne, and many other skin problems. Without a doubt, turmeric root is a powerful medicinal agent, and it can be used in many different situations to treat a vast number of diseases.

Now let's get into those amazing super foods I was telling you about at the beginning of this chapter.

Blueberries: The consumption of fruits and vegetables has been viewed as positive for a long time and is linked to better health conditions related to lifestyle. It has also been suggested that plant-derived foods can also be a link to a decrease in cardiovascular disease, weight gain, diabetes, and mortality rates. These foods not only help you be healthier, but they also make you look better, as they benefit your hair and skin health, and give you more energy to get through your day. Blueberries contain "iron, phosphorous, calcium, magnesium, manganese, zinc, and vitamin K," which in turn are the components of the human bone. A higher intake of these vitamins and minerals can help you maintain bone strength, particularly their elasticity. They also improve calcium absorption and prevent bone fractures.

A single cup of blueberries can provide you with a quarter of your daily vitamin C intake. They can also help people with high blood pressure to lower their levels. Blueberries are also devoid of sodium, making them ideal to healthily stabilize your blood level.

Blueberries! Super Food 101!

Walnuts: Walnuts are incredibly nutritious, providing whoever consumes them with fiber, vitamins, minerals, and healthy fats. Their benefits don't stop there, as they in fact can they do a lot more to increase your health. There have been so many studies and research regarding this particular nut that a walnut conference has been created. Running for 50 years, this conference gathers scientists and experts at UC Davis to discuss any updates and findings in the medical properties of walnuts. The most studied type of walnut is the English walnut, which is what you tend to find at your supermarket. Here are 13 science-based health benefits of walnuts.

Walnuts are rich in antioxidants. Compared to other nuts, walnuts are incredibly abundant in antioxidants. Their antioxidant activity is derived by their high levels of melatonin and vitamin C, which can be found on the skin of a walnut.

Walnuts are a super plant source of Omega-3s. Walnuts contain 2.5 grams of omega-3 fat per 28 grams, making their levels of omega-3 much higher than any other nut available in the market. Omega-3 are essential, healthy fats, which we discussed earlier, and including them in your diet can be extremely beneficial and help you prevent cardiovascular diseases. Walnuts! Super Foods 101!

Quinoa: Quinoa is a gluten-free seed, often mistaken for a grain. It is helpful in providing its consumer with long-lasting energy, and contains all essential amino acids. It is also full of antioxidants, and has anti-inflammatory effects that can benefit your health in the long run. The energy it provides you can also help you be more motivated to exercise.

Cooking quinoa is similar to cooking rice, you just need to mix it with some water, salt, and oil, and wait for it to absorb the boiling water. It is recommended to make extra quinoa when you can, as it is an excellent food to add to your existing meals. You can add it to your eggs or your salad to give yourself a good boost. You can also use it to replace rice in any recipe that might need it, making your meal much more nutritious.

Dark Leafy Greens: Greens such as spinach and kale contain high levels of folate and nitrites. This helps turn your fat-storing cells in fat-burning cells and can be a good element to include in your diet if you are trying to lose weight. They have also been linked with a decrease in the risk of cognitive decline, which will, in turn, help you be more positive and happier to be able to tackle other problems. Leafy greens have anti-inflammatory properties, protecting you from cardiovascular diseases and diabetes. They are also one of the few non-dairy sources of calcium, which can be ideal for those who are vegan or lactose intolerant.

You can add leafy greens into sandwiches or salads or be more creative and mix them with fruits to make a delicious breakfast smoothie. You can also cook them with a clove of garlic in a pan, let them cook over medium health, and add salt to make a delicious and nutritional side salad for your meal.

Avocados: Nearly everyone loves the taste of avocados, and they are a type of food you can easily integrate into any meal. But more than just their smooth taste and texture, avocados are also packed with health benefits. Its monosaturated fat provides you with a good alternative to trans fats. Moreover, avocados can help you absorb the nutrients of other foods better (up to 2% more than if you were eating them without avocados), which is why I'd advise you integrate them to your foods.

They can also help lower the risk of cardiovascular diseases and help stabilize your blood and cholesterol levels. They contain pantothenic acids, which help convert carbohydrates into glucose, therefore giving you more energy to get through your day.

Wild Salmon, Cod, Flounder, Sole, and Trout: Salmon and other wild fish are an enormous source of omega-3 fats, helping you decrease risks of cancer, depression, and cardiovascular diseases. They also contain high levels of protein. It is recommended to buy wild salmon at markets, rather than farm-raised at supermarkets.

Organic Pasture Raised Eggs: Everyone knowns eggs are a gold mine of protein. They contain not only omega 3, but also the vitamin B your body needs. However, regular eggs and organic pasture raised eggs differ in the amount of protein they provide you with. The latter are more costly, but they come from chickens who roam free on their farm and benefit from a healthy, organic diet. This means richer yolks, better tastes, and vitamin A and E for you.

Almond Butter: Contrary to store-bought, processed peanut butter, almond butter contains a lot more nutrients. It has an outstanding amount of monosaturated fats for your health, as well as magnesium, manganese, and copper. Vitamin E, Vitamin B, and riboflavin are also present in it, helping you gain some energy. Double check the label to make sure it is not processed and doesn't contain sugar or oils.

You can use almond butter to make cookies, or to spread of toast. Many people prefer the almond taste to that of peanut butter, as it is much less artificial. You can even grab a spoonful of it and eat it on its own for an energy boost.

Plain Organic Greek Yogurt: aside from just tasting good, yogurt is a great source of protein and calcium. It can also help improve your digestive health. Go to the Greek yogurt section in your supermarket and look for any brand that contains over 20g of protein and under 10g of unprocessed sugar. If it contains live active cultures, even better. This helps to restore the good bacteria in your digestive system.

Throw a Dinner Party

If you like to entertain, why not throw a dinner party? It's fun and who doesn't like to eat. This is the time to show your presentation skills. Think about fun ways to decorate your table. Presentation when serving food is everything. I've seen mediocre food served with such elegance that guests just couldn't stop talking about how great dinner was and how much they enjoyed the food. It's a visual thing, and it works! Use props like fancy tablecloths and placemats, napkins with dignity and grace, and the champagne bucket from heaven. You must think outside the box on this stuff. Almost anything you can conceptualize can be performed. Look at magazine pictures and articles, shop at different funky sorts of stores. Used shops, elegant high-end shops, one of a kind shops.

Get ideas and wow your guests. It can be endless fun.

Grow your own veggies:

Depending on where you live, there are lots of choices of what you can grow, and it is not that difficult. Ever tasted a home-grown tomato? Mmmmm, delicious and sweet-tasting, nice soft outer skin, and a finish that will make you smile. And that bright red or yellow color! You know how you buy those hard and waxy feeling tomatoes at the local big chain grocery store. They are so old, and hard I don't think they are even tomatoes any longer. They have a pinky washed out look and lack the bright red, and tasty experience home-grown will provide.

All you need is a small plot of earth. Pick up some planter mix if you think you'll need it and get those seeds in the ground. Or, if you prefer, just buy the little pots of a variety of veggies at any local grocery or even ninety- nine cent stores. Gardening is Zen-like and watering too. It is so much fun to see the new little guys when they sprout from their seeds. "Hello little one. Welcome to the world!"

Recipes for A Healthier Mindset

Raspberry Chicken Lettuce Wraps

Ingredients:

1 cup of raspberries, washed

2 tbsp of olive oil

1 tbs of white wine vinegar

1 tsp of Dijon mustard

2 tbsp. of minced scallions

2 cooked chicken breasts, cut into cubes

4 cups of chopped lettuce

Directions:

Whisk together the raspberries with the olive oil and the vinegar in a medium-sized bowl. Add the mustard and some salt and pepper to taste. Add the scallions to the mix to make a vinaigrette. Toss in the chicken to the vinaigrette to make into a salad. Arrange the lettuce on individual plates and place the chicken over it before serving.

Morning Yogurt Boost Supreme

I love this one to start out my day. It is healthy, easy to throw together, and delicious.

Get yourself a large cereal bowl and get ready for some fun. Throw in about a half cup of fresh Blueberries, as many Walnut Halves as you want and cover it with some high-powered Plain Yogurt. (You can cheat if you like and use a fruity flavored yogurt.)

Mix it up a bit and dig in. This is one of those treats that I never want to end, but invariably, the empty bottom of the bowl is reached. Time to get that body moving!

Delicious 3 Bean Salad

Ingredients:
1 Lb. fresh green beans cooked al dente
1 Lb. fresh Yellow Wax Beans (same)
1 Lb. cooked Dark Red Kidney Beans
1 Lge. Green Pepper sliced thinly
2 Lge. Red Onions sliced thinly
½ Cup Salad Oil of choice
¾ Cup White Vinegar
½ Cup Sugar
¼ Tsp of Black Pepper
1 Tbsp. of Salt

Directions:
Mix the sugar, vinegar, oil, salt & pepper until dissolved. Drain green beans & wax beans. Do not drain kidney beans. In a large bowl, mix all the ingredients together. Refrigerate for overnight.

Tender Green Salad with Strawberries, Cucumber & Basil

Ingredients:
- 2 tbsp. of walnut oil or extra virgin olive oil
- 2 tsp. of white wine vinegar
- 1 tsp of honey
- 1/4 tsp. of salt
- 1/8 tsp. of black pepper
- 1/2 a head of butter, Boston or bib lettuce. Tear the leaves out (should leave 5 cups)
- 6 large strawberries, cut in fours
- 1/4 cucumber, slice thinly into half moons
- 2 tbsp. of pistachio nuts, toasted and coarsely chopped
- 4 large fresh basil leaves, torn

Directions:
- In a small bowl, whisk the oil of your choice with the vinegar, honey, salt, and pepper. Use this as dressing
- In a separate large bowl, place your lettuce, and drizzle it with half of your dressing. Toss the mixture.
- Use four salad plates to divide the lettuce and arrange it with the cucumbers and strawberries. Top it off with pistachios, basil, and the remaining dressing.
- This pairs well with grilled chicken breast and grilled pita bread and works as an entrée.

Special Bonus Recipe

Mothers Home Cooked Lemon Bread

Ingredients:
1 ½ Cups Flour
1 Cup Sugar
1 Teaspoon Baking Powder
2 Tablespoons Lemon Rind Grated
½ Teaspoon Salt
½ Cup Pecans Chopped
½ Cup Milk
6 Tablespoons Oil of choice
2 Eggs

Directions:

In a large bowl, mix all ingredients together until smooth but save back ¼ of Sugar. In a separate bowl, squeeze the juice of 2 lemons and add the held back sugar and mix together.

In an oiled and floured bread pan, bake at 350 for 30 to 45 minutes monitoring carefully. Be sure the inside is cooked thoroughly by inserting a slim knife or other item. Should pull out without dough sticking.

When nearly done, pull from oven and pour the Lemon & Sugar mix over loaf.

This will become a wonderful and amazing glaze topping. Cook for about 15 minutes more after adding the glaze but monitor carefully so as not to burn. Enjoy!

The Perfect Recipe

1 Cup friendly words
2 Heaping cups of understanding
A generous amount of time and patience
A pinch of warm personality
A dash of humor
Spice of Life

Measure words carefully while adding heaping cups of understanding. Sift together 3 times before using. Make a smooth sauce, not too thick. Cook on front burner keeping the temperature low.

DO NOT BOIL! Use generous amounts of time and patience. Add a dash of love and a drop of humor. Season to taste with Spice of Life. Serve in individual portions. Best when made by a good mixer.

CHAPTER 6: CONSCIOUSNESS AND MINDFULNESS

Step Six: Be in the moment

We've discussed mindfulness through this book. You might have tried practicing it before, or you might be brand new to the idea. Mindfulness can be extremely beneficial to any of us, and while it might be hard to get into, we can get better at it with time.

This chapter will focus on what mindfulness is. How can you integrate mindfulness and meditation in your regular routine? Is there a point in doing so? This chapter will guide you through all those questions and allow you to see what has made the concept of mindfulness so popular.

What is Mindfulness

Mindfulness is often linked to meditation, or to any other relaxing activities. But in actuality, meditation is only one of the means to be mindful, but it is certainly not the only way.

"...a moment-to-moment awareness of one's experience without judgment. In this sense, mindfulness is a state and not a trait. While it might be promoted by certain practices or activities, such as meditation, it is not equivalent to or synonymous with them."

We can see then that the practice of meditation or other activities can bring a person to a mindful state of mind. It is not a quality or personality trait, and it is important to note that people are not born mindful. Being aware of yourself and your surroundings can allow you to be impartial, which is the essence of mindfulness. Non-judgmental self-reflection can be extremely crucial, especially in a world in which opinions and commentary are present in social media.

"The awareness that arises from paying attention, on purpose, in the present moment and non-judgmentally."

Practitioner and academic theory use this definition to describe mindfulness, and those who practice it aim to feel this way. Beyond just awareness, our senses encourage us to focus on the here and now, a concept that people who practice meditation on a regular basis will be familiar with.

I know it may seem we have been over some of this information before. However, this is intentional. If you read this book all the way through, you will find that you know the process and should be able to apply the principles set out here without even thinking about it. This is why the information given here is so very important for your life and for your future.

Here are eight practical tips to help you get a more positive mindset.

1.   Repeat positive affirmations to yourself

2.   Learn to appreciate good things, even if they seem insignificant

3.   Learn to find the positive in a bad situation

4.   Learn from your mistakes, and think of them as a lesson

5.   Talk positively rather than negatively

6.   Make your breakdowns into breakthroughs

7.   Stop focusing on past mistakes and learn to pay attention to the present.

8.   Surround yourself with friends, mentors, and coworkers who encourage you and support you through hard times.

Consciousness through Mindfulness

Do you ever feel more aware than you usually are, as if you could tune into the people and objects in your environment and perceive then under a completely different light? Or have you had moments of heightened awareness in the middle of a dream, where you can feel yourself consciously making a decision for yourself? Have you ever felt so close to someone, so intimate and compassionate that you could almost think of what they were thinking, and feel what they were feeling?

These are the kind of moments that allow us to experience a different, more profound way of thinking and of perceiving reality. The awareness you feel in those moments can be applied in your regular life and can help you live out your days in a more conscious and connected way.

Being in the now

If you've experienced these moments of awareness, you might have noticed that you start becoming a lot more perceptive of the present moment. Think of it as focusing the lens of a camera: you narrow the depth of field on the lens in order to perceive a particular object more sharply. Similarly, awareness makes you see the world in a clearer way.

Becoming more aware of what you're doing, and by consequence of what surrounds you, you allow your consciousness to make decisions, rather than your subconscious. You can notice this in daydreams, in which you can get so lost in the images your brain creates, or on the thoughts and feelings you're lingering on, that you fail to perceive what is actually happening in your environment. Consciousness can help you be more perceptive of the physical world, but also of the non-physical world.

Even then, we tend to neglect our consciousness. Most of us tend to focus on our thoughts, daydreams, and everyday concerns. But consciousness works like a muscle: the more you exercise it, the more you practice it, the stronger it becomes. This allows you to be more conscious, with less effort.

Being conscious means you have to put aside some things in other to fully experience your immediate surroundings, but it doesn't necessarily mean you stop thinking or feeling. Think of it as a drive in a car: if you are more aware of your thoughts and feelings, you can navigate them better, and even choose which thoughts and feelings you want to have.

Activating consciousness

You can experience consciousness anywhere and at any time. You can even try certain exercises in order to activate your consciousness.

Start by becoming aware of you reading these words. Then, move on to focus on the pace and intensity of your breathing, or even the way your body feels sitting in a chair or lying in bed. Pay attention to the sounds and smells around you; try to discern what they are. Perhaps turn your head to take a look at the light in the room or the color of the object closest to you. Acknowledge any person or animal in your vicinity. Don't worry too much about labeling, but simply focus on perceiving it as the present. Spend a few minutes doing this.

You will notice that you will begin to think more, be it about this book, about a conversation you had, or about something that happened. Make a note of the way you're feeling right now. Do you feel anxious or tensed? Or maybe you feel slightly more active and attentive? These feelings can be a source of motivation, in the same way bouncing your leg can motivate you to stand up and take a walk. Don't let these feelings distract you but perceive them.

Your consciousness is what perceives the emotions you feel. You can direct this consciousness to your exterior, like what you did for your environment, or for your interior, like what you did for your feelings. Perceiving things means you have to think about them; it is not enough to simply see them or feel them.

Consciousness beyond body & mind

As you can see, the exercise you just participated in can allow you to be in touch with your consciousness and notice that there is more going on in your mind besides errand thoughts and feelings. In other words, consciousness can be described as an out of body experience, in which you notice absolutely everything.

Try this exercise again. After a few times, you will notice that the observer you become through consciousness is always the same, even if your actual thoughts and feelings are different.

The Potential for Developing and Enhancing Consciousness

We all have the potential to develop consciousness, each and every one of us. It is just a matter of discovering that potential. The outcome of consciousness has very different names. Some might call it "enlightenment," or maybe "awakening," but it is all the same thing. When they reach these outcomes, people will go on to create artistic masterpieces, write moving music, make amazing scientific discoveries, etc. This speaks for the incredible potential of the human spirit if we only attain this stage of consciousness.

This consciousness is what connects us to "the spiritual source." It helps us connect to each other, to other living things, across time and space. Developing and experiencing consciousness is a way for you to take part in a "greater spiritual reality" and makes our lives worth living.

Mindfulness

Mindfulness is a term that is similar to consciousness. It refers to the process of focusing on experiences happening around you, a process that can be done through meditation or other activities. It is described by many as the ability to be present at the moment, and to reach complete awareness of your surroundings and your actions, without feeling overwhelmed by the information you're taking in.

Anyone is capable of being mindful, but it is something that has to be practiced daily in order to develop it to its full potential.

Being mindful is the act of bringing awareness to the things you are directly experiencing. This can be done through your sense, your thoughts, or your feelings. Studies have actually shown that mindfulness, practiced over long periods of time, can rearrange the structure of your brain in a positive way.

Mindfulness and meditation

People who practice meditation describe as the act of exploring your mind, instead of just a state you aim to attain. It doesn't mean your mind and brain need to be completely free of thought, but rather that every thought you have is important and purposeful. It means being in touch with all your feelings and emotions to understand them better.

When you stop passing judgment on your thoughts and start being more curious about the way they are generated, you are practicing mindfulness meditation. You can attain mindfulness not only through meditation but also through body scans, breathing exercises, etc. You just have to remember to be kind to yourself about your thoughts.

The Basics of Mindful Practice

Put some distance between yourself, and your reactions, and take time to think about your actions mindfully.

1.   Set aside some time. Meditation doesn't have to be conducted in a specific place, with specific props and equipment. Having a space and a time set aside for meditating is more than enough.

2.   Observe the present moment as it is. Don't quiet your brain or try to tune out every thought you may have. Your goal isn't to be calm; it is to be able to focus on the present, on your feelings, and on your surroundings, without passing judgment.

3.   Let your judgments roll by. If you feel yourself judging a specific thought or feeling you experience, make a mental note of it, and reflect on it later.

4.   Return to observing the present moment as it is. If you get lost or carried away in your own thoughts, simply make yourself go back to the present moment. This can often happen, but remember to be mindful and bring yourself back.

5.   Be kind to your wandering mind. If you do wander off, don't blame yourself for it, and don't judge your mind. Recognize when it happens, and gently bring your mind back to the present moment.

Of course, these things are easier said than done.

Fortunately, practice can go a long way in helping you master these basics and obtain results from it.

Stress Mental Health and Mindfulness

More and more Americans every year are reporting that they feel extremely stressed, according to The American Psychological Association. As researchers continue to understand the ability for stress to precipitate mental and physical ailments, the importance of research-backed stress reduction strategies increases.

Stress can, at times be beneficial. It can motivate us to study for a test, and it helped our ancestors survive the threat of dangerous wildlife.

The challenge is that ongoing stress, trauma, and adverse life events impact our ability to stay resilient and over time we may find ourselves developing anxiety, depression, health challenges and addictive behaviors to deal with the chronic stress we are experiencing internally. While mental illness is the foremost contributing factor to disability in the United States, research demonstrates that many mental health challenges are preventable, and intervention treatments are often highly effective.

However, no matter what the situation is, the ability to return to a parasympathetic, calm state once the stressor is over, is a leading component of good health. As our world speeds up, it's up to us as individuals to take the time that we need to slow down. Think of mindfulness as an exercise for your brain. Just as physical exercise is a component of overall health, so too is mindfulness and meditation. As we continually find more efficient solutions to our everyday problems, sometimes it's nice to have a reminder that going back to basics, and focusing on our breath, will help keep us evolving.

Alleviating Stress with Natural Alternatives

The use of meditation to reduce stress has been demonstrated in its ability to change the perception and build resilience to stressors. In a population of student athletes, one review assessed three intervention studies, each included 7-12 mindfulness sessions, around an hour in length, over a few weeks. They summarized that mindfulness reduced perceived stress and negative thoughts. Another study analyzed the effects of an eight-week mind-body program. Results showed that compared to the control group, the meditators had improved resilience and emotional intelligence.

Evidence is demonstrating that a regular meditation practice may increase awareness of emotional responses and improve one's stress response, reducing the ability for stress, and its debilitating effects, to overcome you.

This was noted in a group of ER nurses, a population known for having high amounts of stress due to a high-pressure job. After using a biofeedback meditation program for four 30 minutes sessions over one month, the nurses reported significant improvements in their ability to manage their stress.

Stress and Deep Breathing

One of the first things that are affected when we are chronically stressed is our breathing. A nervous system that is stressed causes rapid, shallow breathing. When we form a chronic pattern of rapid, shallow breathing, then we create a nervous system that is operating under chronic stress, which, in turn, affects your mental and physical health.

Breathing is one of the best ways to get access to our Stress System (the Fight/Flight/Freeze system) and help it get back to a relaxed state where optimal health occurs.

Take a breath in right now. Are you breathing into your chest or into your belly? If you notice your chest expanding when you breathe, then you are likely breathing on a shallow level. Your breath stops at your sternum and doesn't go deeper into your belly, expanding your diaphragm.

Take a minute now to breathe deeply into your belly. While breathing in expand your diaphragm and belly. When you exhale, allow your belly to go back in. This is how we were born to breathe. When you watch a baby breathing, you can see their belly rising and falling.

Deep, slow breathing helps us to move from a chronic stress response back into a state of

BALANCE…because it is a balance that we really want to help us create optimal health.

A nervous system that is in balance is one that is calm and regulated in the face of stress. Keep in mind that it isn't about not experiencing stress because we cannot avoid it. We are all human, after all. Instead, the shift in mindset here is about how we experience stress and changing our nervous system response to stress. If we don't resolve the stress, then it tends to live on and on in our bodies, creating a chronic stress response.

Breath is an incredible tool to help us shift our response to stress and immediately activate the relaxation, rest, and repair part of our nervous system.

Controlling the Chronic Stress Response

Breath is a very ancient tool that only recently has been proven as an incredible healing tool to access the automatic stress response happening in the Autonomic Nervous System. This is the part of our nervous system that we cannot control, and it can go off on a tangent creating high blood pressure, anxiety, sweaty palms, panic responses, as well as pain and ill health. The inability to return to a parasympathetic nervous system state is the critical message reported by Americans. This can have significant consequences on health, having the potential to bring about high blood pressure, stroke, and circulatory complications. It is estimated that $30 billion/year is lost from work-related stress, with work being the largest source of stress. Although people seem to be aware of their high levels of stress, the biggest obstacle to change is noted as a lack of money, energy, or confidence to improve.

Stress Response Through Good Habits

The best way to develop a new habit is to tie it into a habit you already have. You can do it during meetings or working on the computer. Many of us hold our breath when hurrying to type emails and documents. You can also do it while on your smartphone on social media! You can also practice more regulated deep breathing every day.

Optimal Health Through Deep Breathing

The science and research indicate that deep breathing and mindfulness practices help to decrease inflammation and improve immune system regulation, metabolism, emotional regulation, and improve anxiety and depression symptoms too. It also helps with cravings and optimal brain focus and functioning.

One recent study followed clinically diagnosed anxiety patients during an eight-week mindfulness meditation program and showed improvements in anxiety and depression scores post-intervention and at the three-month follow-up. We are still uncovering the exact ways in which meditation reduces anxiety, but studies are showing certain areas of the brain become active during meditation that relates to the ability to better control emotional responses.

In addition, frequent mindfulness practice is connected to:

- Decreased cortisol levels (stress hormone)
- Increased dopamine levels (feel-good hormone)
- Increased immune function
- Decreased cardiovascular risk factors (lower blood pressure)
- Decreased inflammation (by changing histones and methyl groups sitting on top of genes that reduce inflammation)
- Optimization of the enzyme telomerase (which slows the aging process)

Time to Take Charge

It's time for us to take control of our emotional responses to difficult situations. As counterintuitive as it may seem, the best way to reduce stress may not be to work harder and push through it. By acknowledging the overwhelming feeling stress can cause, and removing oneself from the situation, we can take time away and return to the task with a different perspective. Using this time out to establish a regular meditation practice may be one important solution to improve our quality of life.

Even though researchers are still establishing the

mechanisms underlying meditation's effects on the brain, the benefits of the practice are becoming widely acknowledged in the scientific community. In our technologically advanced and high-stress society, the diagnoses of depression, anxiety, and other mental illnesses are increasing. By sharing meditation research and products with you, we hope to provide you with tools that can help you and your families live with good health, happiness, and peace.

CHAPTER 7: THE ROAD AHEAD

Step Seven: A little at a time will do.

Notice that you are advancing but do not be concerned you are not there yet.

You will nudge your mind step by step a little closer each day.

Sudden uninvited thoughts that enter your mind about what to make for dinner tonight or what to wear in the morning are, in this usage, unproductive.

Uh oh!   Leaky pipe!   Toolkit!   Fixed!

So, when you go to your job, you are focused, so why not in your personal life? Get the picture? Always choose "Productive" thoughts and note the improvement in your daily life.   Unproductive thoughts and words are a waste of your precious time and will drag you down. Ineffective thoughts have no value!

Don't be surprised to find that you feel different. Before long you will begin to notice, slowly at first, that the things you are doing are working and you will love the results.

Remember to take time for you and time with family. Family is the most important thing in the universe. Don't just play but rather give playtime a priority rating in your life. Create music, artwork, or the written word. There is love energy in creativity.

This is what is happening when you begin to notice your new positive mindset hard at work.

Positive Attitudes and how to identify them:

• Don't be afraid of adversity

• Be satisfied with what you have instead of whining for more

• Enjoy things you didn't expect, even if it differs from what you wanted

• Speak positively to motivate your peers

• Change the tone of a conversation by smiling more

• Be friendly, even to strangers

- Don't give up if you fail once. Keep getting up, even when you fall down often

- Be energetic and uplift the people around you

- Remember that the people in your life will always be more important than the possessions you have

- Find ways to be content with the little things you have

- Be happy, even if you know you won't win

- Be happy and proud of the successful people around you

- Look beyond your bad circumstances and think positively about the future

- Again, smile

- Don't hesitate to compliment people, even if you don't them

- Praise other people for their hard work, and be genuine about it

- Try making other people's days better

- Don't complain about your current situation, even if you think it's unfair

- Don't let negative people around you make you feel down

- Give without expecting to get something out of it

- Stay true to yourself

We have now laid the foundation for a positive mindset, but you must be wondering: what is the point? Why should I put so much effort into being positive?

Having a positive mindset can impact your life in wonderful ways and can even change it for the better. Combined with awareness and integrity, it helps you not only increase your quality of life but also start thinking of your life in a more positive way.

The importance of developing the right thoughts

A positive mindset and the benefits that come along with it will always be dependent on the thoughts in your mind

No, this doesn't mean only thinking happy thoughts or ignoring the negative feelings you might have. That is unhealthy. A positive mindset means adopting a perspective in which both your positive and negative thoughts are present, and making the conscious decision of applying that perspective in a positive way to help yourself feel more confident and cheerful, no matter the situation you're in.

You won't always be happy. Negative emotions and difficult events happen, and there is no way to make them disappear completely. A positive mindset acknowledges this.

Mindfulness, and the positive mindset that it generates, are about being in control of how you react in any situation. It will not allow you to control your emotions, nor to tune out negative thoughts, but it will help focus on positive emotions instead and make rational decisions that will make you happy.

Letting yourself sink into a negative mindset will do nothing but make you feel even worse. You will feel powerless and hopeless, and this will influence your decisions in a negative way. It could cause you to react harshly, or to make impulsive decisions instead of coming up with helpful solutions.

When you focus on the positive and put effort into thinking of a good solution to your problems instead of wallowing in self-pity, you can lead a happier life in which you have the power to make yourself feel better.

If you want to be successful, whether it is at work or in a relationship, you need to be able to recognize opportunities and to go after them. As you know, these opportunities aren't offered to you on a silver platter, and they are often packed with difficulties. This is where a positive mindset can come a long way. With practice, you can adopt a new way of thinking in order to take advantage of those opportunities.

Release your inner negativity

Skepticism has the power to influence your decisions and make you pass on incredible opportunities that could change your life. Allowing yourself to dwell on negative thoughts will only make you even more skeptical. You will start to hesitate, and you will lose confidence and trust in yourself. Negativity is the main obstacle between you and success.

The best way to get rid of negativity is to replace it with something much better, and this is where having a positive mindset comes into play. Once you take control of your mind and thoughts, you are able to focus on the positive aspects of a situation. Mindfulness can help you gain control of your thoughts, and with this power, you can align them to something that makes you happy. Don't let negativity stop you from achieving your full potential.

Start thinking differently with mindfulness techniques. If you are feeling too stressed or distracted while working on an important task, take a moment to slow down and calm your mind. Breathing exercises and brief meditation sessions can help rid your mind of negative thoughts. Once you take a deep breath, you will be ready to face any problem.

By practicing mindfulness, your brain will be able to identify and filter out negative thoughts and replace them with positive ones.

For years, your brain has been trained to focus on the negative whenever you face a difficult situation, but it is possible to train it again to adopt a more positive mindset. Once you are able to focus on silver linings and small positive things, you will be able to get out of negative situations much more easily.

Now, think about your thinking patterns. Focus on the way your thoughts flow. Do you tend to jump from one thought to a negative outcome of that thought? Do you find yourself in a cycle of negative thinking? Being cynical will not help you attain your goals, which is why you need to have more awareness in order to make the decisions that can lead you to success.

Once you identify your pattern of thinking, you will be able to alter the pattern and think more positively.

If you manage to identify the cynical cycle you're stuck in, you can break free from it by using the tools this book has provided you with: meditation, diet, breathing exercises, etc.

If you are still experiencing difficulties, try finding the opposite of the negative thought you're having. Picture the worst-case scenario, and then turn it around completely. Then, you will know what it's like to have a positive mindset. Furthermore, if you think about the steps you need to take in order to make that positive thought happen, you can make it a reality.

Start thinking about the things that cause you stress and anxiety. Remember that these emotions are what is holding you back from great opportunities and that you can help reduce them by identifying the cause. Once that cause is identified, think about what kind of thought pattern you could have in order to think positively about that situation. Be confident, think about the best-case scenario, and slowly let go of any anxiety.

Patterns of thinking are a habit, and it is normal for your mind to slip and start thinking of them again. It is important to remember that this is a process and that you need to put effort into consciously changing your way of thinking. When the habit of thinking positively sets it, it will be hard to change it back.

Good cheer is contagious

Be kind to the people around you. Acts of kindness and goodwill not only make the people around feel good, but it also makes you feel good as a result. Small actions that might represent a low effort on your part can bring both you and other people happiness and put a stop to negative thinking.

Feelings of anxiety or stress can be caused by any interaction you might have, which is why is it important to reflect on your pattern of thinking instead of just avoiding specific scenarios. Be kind to the people around you, make them happy, and suddenly, a meeting with your boss or an important discussion with your significant other won't seem so terrifying.

Be here now

Sometimes, changing your thought pattern isn't enough. It must actually bring you happiness, and you have to put effort into feeling happy about what is happening in the present moment.

Don't push the practice of mindfulness to next Monday, or to the next time you have to make a New Year's resolution. Get started right now and take a step towards being aware of your thoughts and feelings. Practice the exercises suggested in this book and allow yourself to gain awareness of your surroundings.

Once you gain that awareness, you can start redirecting your thoughts to more positive things. Once this becomes a habit in your life, your subconscious will no longer be the one in charge of your decisions. Your consciousness, your brain, will be the one filtering negative thoughts and allowing you to take a more balanced approach when solving problems.

Relationships and the human family

Relationships are at the center of many of our lives. They impact our health, our career, and most of our decisions. This is why it is incredibly important to surround yourself with supportive people and to maintain relationships with people who give you energy, who motivate you, and who add purpose with your life. After all, you are dedicating these people your time and attention, and you should be able to gain something positive from it. Friends and family are the people you can reach out to when you find yourself isolated, or when you are confused about an important decision. Making them happy and lending them a helping hand and a shoulder to cry on is a way to make them and yourself happy, and will ensure that they do the same for you when you need it. Positivity means being kind to yourself, and this becomes a lot easier when the people around you are kind to you too. If you find yourself in trouble with regards to a friendship or a relationship, put effort into fixing it if you feel these people will be valuable to you in the long run.

Many people have studied the science of love, and we have even spoken about it in earlier chapters, but it is important to remember that the chemistry involved in love is complex. The scientific basis is not enough for a lot of people to explain the way they feel about another person, and many believe that it rounds down to more than just chemistry. Don't spend too much time worrying about the chemistry of it and focus instead on what that relationship means to you and to the other person in your life.

CHAPTER 8: VISUALIZE SUCCESS!

Step Eight: Visualize each day as one step higher!

If success were easy, we would all be successful. So why are some of us achieving our dreams and the rest of us not so much? Don't be like the Pinball in the popular game that bounces aimlessly from obstacle to obstacle and finally ends up going down the drain. You must be vigilant and set your thought problem markers so you always have self-feedback and can make the necessary corrections in "fixes" along the way. Soon enough, this will happen naturally.

Easy right? And it works! Make it fun to learn and grow.

We all have the power to visualize ourselves where we really want to be. This phenomenon is extremely effective when harnessed and used correctly. You must have a clear picture in your mind as to how your success looks.

A good idea would be to take time out, perhaps in the evening before retiring for the day or if you are a morning person, by all means, get right to it early. Find a place you feel comfortable and continue to use the same space each day and do not skip a day. This is your private "meeting" with your corporation, your chain of stores, whatever your dream is. Then, use your higher mind to visualize every little detail about where you want to be and be there!

Picture yourself having the best sports team on the planet, the most efficient software company or the most popular modeling agency. All you have to do is clear your mind of everything that does not pertain to your dream.

If you hold your "meetings" in the morning, use affirmations as the day progresses. If your meeting was at the end of your day before retiring, the last thing you think about before falling asleep should be your affirmation and in either case, recite your affirmation over several times, so it is the last thing you think about. This only takes a few minutes but will make a tremendous difference in your journey to success. Self-affirmations have been used to treat people with depression in a successful and long-lasting way. What's more, affirmations may also help to mitigate the effects of stress. Once you have more self-esteem, your positive affirmations will be more effective than ever before.

When you think of the goal that you want to achieve, it's only natural to think of all of the obstacles that will come your way as well. Do not allow these obstacles to become so big in your mind that they inhibit you from moving forward. If you can picture yourself achieving your goal, you will achieve it! Rather than creating larger than life limitations in your mind and dwelling on everything that will hold you back, envision yourself victorious.

Use Affirmations Daily: An affirmation is a statement that will help you overcome any obstacle and barriers that negative thoughts put in your way. Repeat them often enough, and you will see positive changes taking shape. Take a look at the word "affirmation." You see that word "Firm" in there? It means to tighten or strengthen. To be steady and strong. The art of being unyielding to obstacles and barriers. Affirmations are just what the doctor ordered!

When you recite your affirmations either aloud or quietly to yourself, every cell in your body will listen to and accept the ideas of love and strength you are building.

If you are an individual with especially low self-esteem, the most effective way to use affirmations is to work on your self-esteem first and then begin the affirmations. Self-esteem is your opinion of yourself and your potential.

When your inner voice whispers to you that you "can't," use your Toolkit and kick that word right out of the picture.

Then, be sure to replace that negative word with a "positive" one. Your affirmations are taking shape. Do this all day every day, and soon you will be reciting your affirmations and climbing higher each day.

Here are seven things you can do each day to be in the positive and not the negative thoughts

1. **Start your day with an affirmation** that "firms" up your core positive beliefs.

If you begin your day with a negative emotion, it could affect your entire day negatively. Create an affirmation that represents your plan for the future and repeat it over and over, and soon you will know it by heart. Your mind will hear this, and you will notice a huge difference as you go through your day.

2. **If things don't go your way, find humor in it all.** Remember, there is a balance to life, and this means peaks and valleys. You may truly find your situation comical but either way, be light-hearted, and you will get through it. One more thing, laughter is contagious, so if you are in a group, don't be surprised if the whole room gets the giggles.

3. **Look for the good in every situation.** No matter what happens, there will be good on any given

day. Just wait and see. You have to plow through the obstacles and know that good things will happen every day.

4. **Turn your Breakdowns into Breakthroughs!** If you make a mistake, learn from it. If somebody else makes a mistake and if it reflects on you, learn from it. There is always something revealed with situations like these. Look for that something, and the chances are very good that next time it happens, and it will always happen again, you will be ready for it.

5. **When you trap your inner voice acting up again**, use your Toolkit to grab that leaky thought and toss it right out of there. Then replace that negative notion with a positive one. Easy!

6. **Be in the moment!** It is really the only one you have. Remember that what is happening now is not yesterday or tomorrow but only right now. The future is fluid and always changing, so be here now.

7. **Positive people make positive company!** If you find you are hanging with an individual who brings you down in any way, get rid of them! Life is too short to suffer the depressed masses, and if you operate from a positive position, you will attract the same in good company.

A thought from Winnie the Pooh might be a good idea too. Remember this one?

"You are braver than you believe, stronger than you seem and smarter than you think!"

Hey, that's an affirmation. Just change the "you are's" to "I am's" and you can say it every morning. Thanks, Winnie!

If you are enjoying this book, please take a moment to write a review on Amazon. We would love to hear from you.

How to Visualize Success

Matt Mayberry, a writer for the Entrepreneur, offers a great opening into what visualizing success means:

"I strongly believe in the power of visualization. We must "see that image" in our mind before we ever venture forth to manifest it. Jim Carrey is one of my favorite examples of this. The famous comedian and actor was once a "wannabe." I remember seeing a highlight of his appearance on "The Oprah Winfrey Show" back in 1997, and he spoke about his early days trying to make it in the entertainment business. He was broke and had no future. But he took a blank check and wrote out $10 million dollars to himself for acting services rendered and dated it for Thanksgiving 1995. He said that he carried that check in his wallet at all times and looked at it every morning, visualizing receiving $10 million dollars. Five years after he wrote the check to himself and right before Thanksgiving 1995, he found out that he was going to make $10 million dollars from the movie "Dumb and Dumber." That's the power of visualizing your dreams. That's the power of dreaming. That's the power of relentlessly believing and working toward your vision every single day."

Picture Yourself Where You Want to Be

Get into the habit of picturing yourself where you want to be. Look beyond what your current circumstances are, and visualize your future, and what it should look like. Try to focus on details: if you want a better job, picture yourself at work, on your chair, doing whatever it is that makes you happy. Think your environment through, down to the last detail, to recreate your dreams.

Try making yourself index cards for what your dreams will look like and read them over when you wake up and before going to bed. Imagine yourself in that scenario and let that thought guide your actions through the day. This trigger card is extremely powerful, as it will give you the happiness and motivation you need to make that dream a reality.

Other Stories of Successful Visualization

This might seem completely futile at first, but many successful people have taken up the habit of visualizing their ideal lives, years before actually achieving them. Some people write their dreams down every day, some simply read them, but the principle remains the same: you must be able to picture what success looks like you. Once that is done, it will seem much more attainable, especially if you don't leave out any details to the abstract. When you remind yourself of what your dreams are, you become more focused on making it happen. Trigger cards might not do much for you at first, but it is a step in the right direction.

Do not feel intimidated by it, and do not hold yourself back from dreaming big simply because you think it's unrealistic. Write your dreams down, and they will seem a lot more possible.

Talk to Yourself

Engage in private dialogue with yourself in order to have a clear idea of what you feel. Don't simply think it but try to word what you are feeling. Once you know how to have conversations with yourself and put your thoughts into concise and clear words, it will become much easier to express yourself to others. You can also use this moment to reason with yourself when you are feeling conflicted, to motivate yourself if you are stressed, or simply to rehearse something you are going to say if you begin to feel anxious. And do not forget to tell your negative thoughts to shut up. Do not speak to yourself negatively, but rather use this internal dialogue to make you feel better.

Your Own Personal Perspective

Imagining success is easier for some people than it is for others. Some people can think about their goals and dreams at any point of the day, almost as if It were a daydream.

Think of it as a movie of your ideal life, but always keep in mind that you are in control of this movie and its narrative. The plot, the setting, the characters, the tone… everything is for you, the director, to decide. And don't forget that you are the main character, that the camera is focusing on you, and that, most importantly, the director has the power to get the main character through any tough situation in order to have a happy ending. As the cinematographer and main character, this movie is also shot from your own perspective, meaning that no one else gets to decide what happiness means to you. As the filmmaker, you set your own goals, and you find your own way to attain those goals.

Visualize in Living Color

Going back to the movie analogy, picture yourself

as the art and casting director. Who is in the audience as you give your acceptance speech for your big award? What does the house you live in look like? What kind of pictures are covering its walls? Don't be afraid of detail: it will only make you more motivated.

CHAPTER 9: SUNRISE - SUNSET

Step Nine: If you could choose success over failure, you would not choose failure.

We are all blessed with the most beautiful blue water planet in the Sol System.

Our days are filled with sunshine, and we are surrounded by amazing animal life and greenery suitable for an Emperor. Each second of each minute of each hour of each day is savored, and we give thanks for our abundance. As long as we have air to breath and water to drink, we shall smile and be thankful for the lives we have been granted. Simply being here is a miracle of love.

As we experience each day, we are excited to reach another one. Our days are gifts in and of themselves; however, those of us who feel driven will rise above the clouds in our endeavors and in our dreams. We are in unity in our species, and we are in love in our hearts. In our free will, we will continue to learn and to grow knowing all the while that we are one. As the rain falls in Oregon and the sun warms the desert under blue skies in Arizona, we thrive.

No matter who you are or where you may live, it will always be up to you to keep moving ever upwards, ever forwards to a better life. Our hearts are free to do anything we can dream, and we shall do just that!

Never give up your dreams. Never believe that you can't. Always believe in yourself. You are here now. When you achieve some degree of success, you must keep working hard. Keep doing it! You made a winning formula so now keep it going.

Your success means you'll still have to do the work you were doing that got you here.

It's just a whole lot more fun.

When you have achieved success in your life and have your dreams firmly in your hands, remember your roots. Remember the love of what you did and who you were before you got that success. Don't flaunt it or tell too many people about it. Be discreet and classy. Also, a little humility will go a long way.

Keep in mind that the future is fluid. Keep in reserve who you were when you started your journey. Your success is savored but remember that you were good without it and you can be good again. Above all, do not be surprised that you got what you wanted!

Success and failure share similar qualities, and this is something most people might be quite surprised about.

Failure slingshots you into the darkness of despair and hopelessness while success slingshots you into the blinding light of fame and recognition. Both can be equally intense, and both carry equally serious issues to contend with.

It is wise to understand that neither success nor failure are the absolute end to an ultimate journey. Rather both are merely parts or segments of your overall development as a human being.

The human spirit is incredibly resilient. Despite hearing countless stories and seeing the proof in those who have "been there, done that," we still believe that when we set off to pursue our passions, things will go exactly as planned.

We feel invincible to the odds that things may go differently than how we imagined. But, no matter how much plotting, planning, or research we do, the journey will inevitably look different from the set-in-stone ideas we had regarding how we'd get there. The best-laid plans.

The beauty and challenge of life is that the dots don't connect while you're looking forward. Life is speckled with events, challenges, and rewards that can sometimes seem nonsensical. And, when the outcome of a situation isn't exactly what you expected, you might feel disappointed, even if the outcome is better than what you had in mind.

But there are some serious upsides to having life throw curveballs at you. Here are just a few of the many benefits of not getting exactly what you want:

<u>You will always learn and grow no matter how it</u>

turns out

Talent, intelligence and vision are attributes anyone would like to have, but if you don't have the perseverance to relentlessly pursue your vision, all the talent in the world will serve no purpose. Your ability to persevere will land you opportunities to showcase your natural abilities. It's far more dependable than luck when it comes to being in the right place at the right time and surrounding yourself with the right company.

You may redefine success

A corner office, a Grammy award or a book deal may seem like surefire achievements to let you know you've "made it." But, when those milestones are hard to come by, you learn to appreciate even little victories: a raise at your job, a song you wrote that made a friend cry, or perhaps a publisher agreeing to a meeting with you.

Ultimately, the big things are composed of little things, so each steppingstone will seem like it carries far more weight than you probably imagined.

You learn to seek the unknown

Often, we overestimate what or how much it would take to make us feel happy, successful, or safe. And ultimately, whether it's through money, recognition, or health, that's what we're all after. You don't necessarily want your dream job; you likely just want to be as happy as you imagine you would be if you had your dream job. And sometimes, when we recognize what we want to feel rather than what we want to have, we allow ourselves to be fulfilled in ways we never would be expected.

Time after time, life is a choice and the future is always fluid

We can spend so much time and energy focusing on one possible outcome that we forget why we even wanted it at all. Sometimes, being pointed in another direction provides the opportunity and affirmation we need to know that it's okay to re-evaluate and start again.

Your creativity will continue to grow

Some people don't take no for an answer, not when they want something that could lead them to happiness. Not getting what you want the first time leads you to think outside the box and go off the beaten path to get to your ultimate goal, making you not just successful, but also incredibly innovative.

You will lose your fear of failure

The best thing about rejection is that it will lead you to an important discovery: not getting what you want will not kill you. The world keeps turning, and you are now stronger and wiser when you have to face another problem.

Life is an inspiration

Winning the lottery of life seems to be a tempting option, but when you have to work for your dreams, and others see you making them come true, you become a role model.

You allow the ups and downs in your journey to serve as the inspiration that someone else needs to get what he or she wants out of life. What is life but a series of peaks and valleys?

You will learn to trust, and you will learn integrity

It is often said that there is no such thing as a self-made success because of all the effort and investments others have to make for you to get you there. Build solid relationships.

When you don't get what you want, the invitation is there to pull away from people. However, those who are committed to success know that leaning on others is the quickest way to get up after a fall. And, it's the surest way to ultimately "make it."

Learn your strengths and weaknesses

Learn to know yourself. You know who you are in the perfect conditions, when there are no problems or issues for you to worry about or wallow into negativity. It is important, however, that you also know who you are under unfavorable circumstances.

Finding out who we are, gives us the opportunity to build on our strengths and nip our weaknesses in the bud before the stakes are too high, and there's much more to lose. Are we all not but students of life?

Acknowledging complacency

Not getting what you want, whether something big or small, pushes you out of your comfort zone. Ultimately, that's where you have to get comfortable living to make a noticeable difference in your life or in the world.

Lesson Number One: Work Smart!

A roadblock can slow us down long enough to recognize the surplus of energy we sometimes devote to working hard, but not working smart. The downtime you get from a "no" can help you re-strategize and re-approach a challenge with a new perspective.

Find wisdom everywhere

Anger, frustration, and fear are all emotions that can be seriously toxic to your success, wellbeing, and relationships. But, when you don't get what you want, you learn to use anger and turn it into drive.

Frustration can turn into vision, and fear can turn into courage. These are emotions that reflect growth and can be used productively.

What a story

At the end of your life, it won't be the times you won that are the most interesting, inspiring, or exciting. Someday, it may very well be the struggle that possesses the sweetest part of your success and the stories you want and with a little luck, will be asked to tell.

Well, looks like we're closing in on the end of this book. If you enjoyed reading it, please leave a review on Amazon. We always love hearing from you.

It's a Long Way to The Top

I think the most glaring and prevalent set of stories regarding handling success would be to look back at the history of "successful" rock bands since the 1960's. The one thing they all have in common is drugs and alcohol. When interviewed, most band members say the exact same thing.

Basically, that they were not present to life. What do I mean by that? Well for one thing, most of them were very young and in almost all cases there was substance abuse in massive proportions. But there was something more. Something more sinister and clandestine. They say things like, "we weren't ready for success!" Not ready for all the attention. Not prepared for all the responsibility. For having an obligation to actually show up at a certain time and place ready to perform and ready to repeat this process time and time again without being late or making any musical mistakes. Not even close to ready for the responsibility. The Rock world is so free-spirited during the times before hitting it big, that the main line of chatter I hear is that they had no idea that being in a band could produce success.

That's it in a nutshell! A closer look shows something extraordinary. All of the band members in nearly all of the bands talked about nothing else when they began their journey as bandmates.

They all wanted it and then acted so surprised when they got it. Immaturity? Stupidity? No, I think that in the end, it simply comes down to not present to life. They really didn't believe that what they were doing would ever amount to anything more than having fun and getting laid.

They just weren't ready for it, and it was there the entire time. Now I know that in all actuality, most bands, garage bands, are not even qualified for success in the entertainment world but some are and while that creates a distinction between the two, blazon incompetence is prevalent on both sides. When you add driving their expensive sports cars into Oak Trees at high speed and incomprehensible infidelity to the mix, all of which while clutching a quart bottle of Jack Daniels in one hand well then nothing surprises me.

Movie stars, comedians and politicians often find the dizzying height intoxicating as well and lose their sense of balance.

This brings us right back to what we have been covering in this book. Developing the best **mindset for growth and positive thinking to achieve success in life and live your dreams.**

And, while there are so many ways to talk about it, the one thing you need is to learn how to control your thoughts. <u>We all have our inner voice. How we respond to it is the key.</u>

Finally, if you found this book useful in any way, a review on Amazon is always appreciated! Thank you very much, and best wishes on your journey to a growth and positive thinking mindset!

Lightning Source UK Ltd.
Milton Keynes UK
UKHW022229251022
411098UK00003B/94

9 781513 674070